Lines of Descent

The W. E. B. Du Bois Lectures

Lines of Descent

W. E. B. Du Bois
and the Emergence of Identity

Kwame Anthony Appiah

 Harvard University Press

CAMBRIDGE, MASSACHUSETTS
LONDON, ENGLAND · 2014

Library of Congress Cataloging-in-Publication Data

Appiah, Anthony
    Lines of descent : W. E. B. Du Bois and the
emergence of identity / Kwame Anthony Appiah.
        pages   cm
    Includes bibliographical references and index.
    ISBN 978-0-674-72491-4 (alk. paper)
    1. Du Bois, W. E. B. (William Edward Burghardt),
1868–1963.   2. Education—Philosophy.   3. African
Americans—Education.   4. African American
intellectuals.   5. Intellectuals—United States.
6. Identity (Philosophical concept)   I. Title.
LB875.D83A67   2014
973.04960730092—dc23
    [B]   2013030761

Book design by Dean Bornstein

For my sisters, their spouses, and their children—
a family in diaspora

CONTENTS

His triumph is a triumph not of himself alone,
but of humankind . . .

   —W. E. B. Du Bois, "The Superior Race"

Introduction

ON November 3, 1958, W. E. B. Du Bois returned to his alma mater in Berlin to accept a diploma. He was ninety at the time; both he and the institution had endured considerable tumult in the previous half-century. But the building at Unter den Linden 6 seemed little altered. With its Palladian windows and Corinthian pillars, the late-baroque facade revealed its mid-eighteenth-century origins as a palace for a Prussian prince. At the turn of the nineteenth century, Friedrich Wilhelm III had placed the elegant building in the hands of his energetic minister of education, Wilhelm von Humboldt, and in 1809 the Berliner Universität, which came to be named for its royal patron, enrolled its first students. After the Second World War, the German Democratic Republic renamed it the Humboldt University, for Wilhelm and his equally accomplished brother, Alexander; Du Bois would have passed by marble statues of the brothers as he entered.

Inside rose a central stairway clad in red marble, redone in GDR 1950s-style grandeur; a gilt-leafed quote from notable alumnus Karl Marx shimmered above it: "Philosophers have previously only interpreted the world in various ways; the point is to change it." Much of the building had been damaged during the war, but its reconstruction had been a priority for the East German regime, and it had reopened five years earlier, ornamenting what Du Bois described as a city "with new buildings and enterprises, along with ghosts of war and destruction."[1]

On that November day, as a chamber group played Bach, Du Bois stood at the dais of the Senate Hall, a long auditorium with coffered ceilings and grand, arched windows. He may have noticed the large oil paintings of the two Humboldts; he certainly noticed the presence of women, a welcome change since his student days in the early 1890s. The dean of the faculty of political economy, Professor Heinz Mohrmann, commended Du Bois as a "unique role model," and continued:

> Learning, doing research, teaching, and fighting for the application of scientific knowledge: this is what characterizes the many decades of your work. Full of admiration and profound respect, esteemed Professor Du Bois, we recognize the

unique synthesis of scientific knowledge and politically-directed action which distinguishes your entire life. The council of my faculty has therefore unanimously decided, in view of your great scholarly achievements, as well as of your unique contribution to the struggle for the emancipation of Negroes within and outside of the United States, and for your courageous commitment to the preservation of peace, to bestow upon you the degree of Doctor of Economics, *honoris causa*.

After receiving a standing ovation, Du Bois, deeply moved, told the audience, "Today you have fulfilled one of the highest ambitions of my young manhood."[2]

When he entered the university, more than six decades earlier, it was a roiling profusion of schools and ideologies. It was a realm in which cosmopolitan and anticosmopolitan forces contended and sometimes converged, in which concepts of culture, race, nation, individuality, development, and the laws of history were studied and disputed. Youth, Du Bois wrote, seeks "More light!" (quoting, as it happens, Goethe's deathbed cry), and the light to be found at the university, flickering and inconstant, was generated by friction and fire.[3] Du Bois had quit his country for the first time and found himself almost four thousand miles from the world he knew, left to fend for himself in the very heart of the Kaiserreich, at the height of its colonial ambitions. It was the time of his life.

I want to explore, in this study, Du Bois's preoccupations, keeping this intellectual milieu especially in mind. But it will be salutary to begin with a note of caution. Although it is common enough to discuss intellectual genealogies, that metaphor is perhaps too determinate—in the mode of those biblical catalogs of begats—to capture the ferment of the mind. Every intellectual era has its wild yeast, its drifting spores unremarked, unbidden, and (for better or worse) unavoidable. I'm more drawn to a model suggested by the sociologist Robert K. Merton's work on what he called "multiples" in the history of science— independent, simultaneous discoveries of the same thing turn out to be the rule, rather than the exception—and by his notion of the matrix of discovery. Francis Bacon, he thought, had it pretty much right: advances proceed from an accumulating base of knowledge, argument, and insight. Researchers tend to flourish in concerted effort rather than closeted inquiry. There is a reason that science took off in company with the growth of the postal service and has accelerated with telegraph, telephone, and email: the advancement of learning is the work of communities, groups of people in communication.[4] Merton rightly rejected the "false disjunction" between narratives of heroism and narratives of sociological determination. There are heroes, even geniuses, but they do not create their own climate.[5] The fact that Du Bois was the most exceptional of persons does not mean he wasn't also a Representative Man. In this spirit, it seems wiser to speak of matrices, albeit rendered in watercolor rather than in inked intaglios of transmission.

If we think in terms of a matrix from which Du Bois drew and to which he contributed, we'll also be protected from a related distortion. We often imagine teaching as decanting: a scholar pouring wisdom into a pupil. I don't wish to underplay such vertical legacies. Instructors do instruct, at least on good days. But the Mertonian matrix also invites us to think about the horizontal, peer-to-peer aspects of education, which are often at least as important. If we want to know what ideas were "in the air," we can learn, too, from Du Bois's fellow students, whether or not they were rubbing elbows or sharing an inkwell.

The intellectual ferment of Du Bois's *Lehrjahre*—what he called his "Age of Miracles"—cannot be reduced to a small set of doctrines or disputes. There were manifold strains and tensions and tendencies, and not a few were implicated in Du Bois's own project of reclaiming and redefining "the race concept." He sought a model of racial politics that was not Booker T. Washington's model of subordinate development, not the difference-denying universalism of certain humanitarians ("There is no Negro problem," Lyman Abbott, the Boston Congregationalist theologian, insisted loftily in 1890, "only the problem of humanity"), not Bishop Henry Turner's fantasy of separatism and emigration, not even Frederick Douglass's "ultimate assimilation *through* self-assertion."[6] Du Bois was determined to chart another way; and like another great American writer, he encompassed contradiction, contained multitudes. The contradictions in Du Bois's work are never explicitly endorsed, of course, and not always under authorial control. But he does seek often to reconcile tendencies that others thought opposed. So his path would be scientific and romantic; it would be fact-bound and fanciful, liberal and illiberal, collectivist and individualist. It would be ethnocentric and universal in outlook. It would be the story of his singular self—and, in his providential formula, "a message for the world."

~❧~

These days, we would say that William Edward Burghardt Du Bois was an African-American. He would not, of course, have used that term. He would have said that he was an American and a Negro, and, in *The Souls of Black Folk,* his slender masterpiece, he suggested that these descriptions did not fit easily together—that they gave rise to "two warring ideals in one dark body, whose dogged strength alone keeps it from being torn asunder."[7] And what *was* a Negro? Well, that was a question about which Du Bois thought a great deal over many decades. Negroes, he would have said, were a race. Yet *race,* as he knew better than most, is an elusive concept; indeed, he called the story of his own life "the autobiography of a race concept," implying that his own understanding had changed over his long life. At times, as we'll see, he spoke of a vast family, of shared descent and common impulses; at other times, of the inheritors of a common memory; but in the pithiest of his many attempts at definition he said, "The black man is a person who must ride 'Jim Crow' in Georgia."[8] Each of these conceptions has its defenders today. Still, the continuities

in his understandings are as striking as the disconti-
nuities. To appreciate his advances, it is helpful to
bear in mind the ways in which he was not our
contemporary.

Du Bois was born in 1868, the year that *Die Meis-
tersinger von Nürnberg* had its debut; he died in 1963,
when "Surfin' U.S.A" was on the charts. His longev-
ity gives us, I think, a sense that he is more modern
than he really was. It can be startling to realize, for
example, that when Khrushchev gave him the Lenin
Prize in 1959, Du Bois was being honored in the name
of a man two years his junior. If Du Bois sometimes
sounds old-fashioned, it is in part because his fashion
was set in the nineteenth century. Still, even by the
standards of his peers, his prose could be florid. It flows
through his many volumes in a torrent, his distinctive style recognizable from the first sentence of his
most famous book: "Herein lie buried many things
which if read with patience may show the strange
meaning of being black here in the dawning of the
Twentieth Century."[9] More than fifty years later, in
his ninety-third year, Du Bois published the last volume of his trilogy *The Black Flame;* it ends with these
words: "Over his dead body lay a pall of crimson
roses, such as few kings have ever slept beneath."[10]

They were the same self-consciously antiquarian cadences, a sort of literary Puginism. Describing *Souls*, Du Bois ventured another diagnosis: "The style is tropical—African. This needs no apology. The blood of my fathers spoke through me and cast off the English restraint of my training. The resulting accomplishment is a matter of taste. Sometimes I think very well of it and sometimes I do not."[11] Yet Du Bois's abiding concerns retain their urgency, and the challenge he set himself—to come to grips with the social reality of race in a way that both resisted scientific racism and responded to the claims of cosmopolitanism— remains daunting.

Nor is Du Bois's conceit of calling his life story an "autobiography of a race concept" as far-fetched as it first seems. Born and raised in the Massachusetts town of Great Barrington and educated in unsegregated schools, Du Bois was a child when the Compromise of 1877 brought an end to what he was to call the "splendid failure" that was Reconstruction.[12] The bright hopes earlier pinned on institutions like the Freedmen's Bureau (1865–1872) and on direct black participation in the legislative process were already dimming; now they went dark. Among blacks, the result was a certain disaffection with politics as a means of achieving change. As hopes switched to economic development, the emancipationist rhetoric of Frederick Douglass gave way to the practical counsel of Booker T. Washington, who began the work of the Tuskegee Institute in 1881. The voices of back-to-Africa emigrationists grew louder as well.[13] As industrialism led to an influx of blacks to major cities, the "Negro problem" began to conjure urban pathology as well as agrarian backwardness.

Du Bois, graduating at the top of his high school class, began his undergraduate career at Fisk, in Nashville, Tennessee, because a black college was the right place for an African-American, however accomplished, especially one of modest means, dependent for the cost of his education on the philanthropy of strangers. Fisk taught him a great deal—not least, he insisted, how to live in a segregated community. He spent two eye-opening summers teaching poor black kids from East Tennessee in a schoolhouse that was no more than a windowless log hut. His class oration was about Otto von Bismarck, heralding the Prussian statesman's success in making "a nation out of a mass of bickering peoples."[14] Listening to him speak about the Iron Chancellor, his hero, you might have guessed that this young man had a vision of himself as a black

Bismarck; or, perhaps, in a metaphor that would have resonated more deeply for his African-American audience, as a Moses who could lead his people to a promised land.

His achievements at Fisk allowed him to take his bachelor's degree to Harvard, where he earned a second BA two years later in 1890, *cum laude,* and was chosen to give one of the four commencement orations. A year later, he had a Harvard MA in history, working under the tutelage of Albert Bushnell Hart, one of the founders of modern historical studies in the United States. Determined to make a scholarly pilgrimage to Germany, Du Bois petitioned the Slater Fund for a fellowship, firing off a series of letters and testimonials to its head, former President Rutherford Hayes—the very man who gained the White House by agreeing to dismantle Reconstruction. ("To properly finish the education thus begun, careful training in a European university for at least a year is, in my mind and in the minds of my professors, indispensable to my greatest usefulness," the Harvard graduate fellow wrote Hayes.)[15] At last, the fund agreed to provide a stipend for up to two years, and Du Bois, recalling his flush of exhilaration, tells us that, when he left a meeting with President Hayes, the promise of a scholarship secured, he was "walking on air." "I saw an especially delectable shirt in a shop window. I went in and asked about it. It cost three dollars, which was about four times as much as I had ever paid for a shirt in my life; but I bought it."[16] Du Bois, who was always a bit of a dandy, planned to arrive in style.

When Du Bois did arrive at the Friedrich-Wilhelms-Universität (as the University of Berlin was called by the time he got there) he was not disappointed. It had thirty-odd lecture halls on three floors, and its amenities were notably advanced, since it had recently been equipped with electricity, toilets, central heating, and ventilation.[17] Its faculty was the largest of any German university, and included many of the era's most august intellectual figures—a good number of whom we will be meeting in the pages ahead. But after a period of enormous personal and educational growth, his stipend ran out and the Slater Fund turned down his request for a renewal. He had completed a dissertation on systems of farming in the American South, and his advisors at Berlin wrote letters (which Du Bois forwarded to the Slater Fund) explaining that a technicality prevented Du Bois from taking the oral examination that would have made him eligible for a doctorate. A university rule required that doctoral candidates have attended the university longer than Du Bois was able to do.[18]

Nursing his disappointment, Du Bois "dropped suddenly back into 'nigger'-hating America." He wrote to a friend, "I must step, walk, stumble and climb now; for the *Lehrjahre* [learning years] were passed—I fancied—and the *Meisterjahre* [adult years] begun."[19] He took a position at Wilberforce University while he completed another thesis, which would earn him a doctorate in history at Harvard, the first doctoral degree that Harvard had granted to an African-American. This thesis, on the suppression of the African slave trade, was, as it happens, the first dissertation to be published in the Harvard Historical Monograph Series. (In its preface, he was at pains to note that he had tested "the conclusions of this study by the general principles laid down in German universities.")[20] In 1896, the year he published this monograph spanning two centuries of Atlantic history and three continents, the author left his job as a classics professor at Wilberforce to begin a sociological study, at the University of Pennsylvania, of the African-American community of downtown Philadelphia. (Du Bois hadn't liked Wilberforce University much—"What business had I . . . to teach Greek when I had studied men?"—but he met and married Nina Gomer there, a "slip of a girl, beautifully dark-eyed," so he couldn't regard his time in Ohio as entirely wasted.)[21] Three years later, after a period of intensive research, Du Bois published his second book, *The Philadelphia Negro,* which is, arguably, another of his many firsts: the first detailed scientific statistical sociological study of an American community.

By the time that *The Philadelphia Negro* appeared, however, Du Bois himself was no longer a Philadelphia Negro; he had become one of those Georgia Negroes, riding Jim Crow in Atlanta. He had taken a job as professor of history and economics at Atlanta University, which was among the crop of Southern black colleges that sprang up in the years immediately after the Civil War. Founded in 1865 by the American Missionary Association, and supported by the Freedman's Bureau, it was, by the turn of the century, educating black teachers to meet the growing needs of the segregated black schools of the South. The University of Pennsylvania, Benjamin Franklin's institution, was willing to harbor his research: but in the 1890s it could not offer a black man—even one as credentialed as Dr. Du Bois—a job as a professor.

Du Bois spent more than a decade in Atlanta, editing the Atlanta University Studies in the sociology of Afro-America, organizing conferences, teaching and conducting research—research that shows up in the detailed knowledge of the rural South displayed in *The Souls of Black Folk*. Atlanta University was where Du Bois lived out his professorial vocation. And all the time he was publishing. The preface of *The Souls of Black Folk* (he called it a "Forethought") is signed "Atlanta, GA, Feb 1, 1903," which was three weeks before his thirty-fifth birthday. One imagines that on February 2 he began (if he did not finish!) the next work. But simply by posing the sly question, "How does it feel to be a problem?"—one of that book's best-known lines—he had invented a new way of writing about race in America.

When he wasn't writing or teaching or doing research, he was helping to establish organizations of racial uplift: in 1897, he co-founded the American Negro Academy; in 1900, he attended the first Pan-African Conference in London; in 1905, he helped organize the opening conference of the Niagara movement, whose aim was both to ensure black voting rights and to oppose Booker T. Washington's accommodations with segregation. But these institutional efforts of Du Bois's were largely fugitive. The Academy drifted on desultorily for three decades; and the Niagara movement had four conferences and disbanded in 1910. That movement did pave the way, however, for the creation, in 1909, of the National Negro Committee, which was to develop into the National Association for the Advancement of Colored People (NAACP).

It was the NAACP that took Du Bois back out of the South in 1910 to edit its official magazine, *The Crisis,* in New York City and to direct the organization's publications and research (though not before he had added a new genre to his vita, by publishing his impassioned biography of John Brown). He was forty-two, a professor with a curriculum vitae and a list of publications and awards unmatched among African-Americans and equaled by few academics of any color anywhere. Now this scholar in his prime had a national platform on which to speak for the Negro, and he did so there for the next quarter century, until conflicts arose with the organization's integrationist (and integrated) leadership over his statements of support for all-black institutions. He resigned in one of his famous fits of indignation in 1934, at an age—he was sixty-six—when most people of his generation would have been established in a peaceful retirement.

Through these years he shifted slowly further to the left. He had joined the Socialist Party briefly, in 1912, but broke from his mild Fabianism to support Woodrow Wilson. Only in his fifties, after the Bolshevik Revolution, did he begin to read Karl Marx seriously; and, he said, writing in 1940, that Marx came to him then like "a beam of new light."[22] (He was unimpressed by the American Communist Party, however, and its insistence on reducing race problems to class problems. Its official policy of race-blindness, he feared, gave it little appeal to either white workers or blacks.) He returned to Georgia to chair the sociology department at Atlanta University. Within the year he established his place as a major American social historian by publishing *Black Reconstruction,* which gave full due to the agency of the newly enfranchised black Americans in the two decades after the Civil War; he started a new journal, *Phylon;* and naturally he published more books and articles.

When he was forced to retire from Atlanta University in his mid-seventies, he went on working, writing newspaper columns, starting the *Encyclopedia of the Negro.* He continued to organize Pan-African

Congresses; at the fifth Congress, held in Manchester in 1945, he was elected chairman, and met a new generation of Africans agitating for independence (including my father), many of whom went on to help govern their newly freed countries. He returned to the NAACP as a director of special research, from 1944 to 1948, when his activism in peace movements and deepening leftism once again brought him in conflict with the organization. He campaigned for nuclear disarmament, chairing the Peace Information Center, and attracting, inevitably, the attention of Senator Joseph McCarthy and his coterie in Washington. Tried and acquitted in his eighty-third year on charges of being an "unregistered foreign agent," he was denied a passport by the State Department anyway; and so was unable to accept Kwame Nkrumah's invitation to attend the ceremony marking Ghanaian independence. Only as he entered his tenth decade did the Supreme Court finally rule, in *Kent v. Dulles* (1958), that denying American citizens the right to travel because of their political opinions was unconstitutional. Du Bois applied for a passport and promptly began a sort of triumphal world tour.

In addition to that visit to the University of Berlin, he traveled in Europe on both sides of the Iron Curtain; met Khrushchev in Moscow and Mao and Chou En Lai in Peking. (Du Bois could have a blind spot for nonracial forms of domination.)[23] Shirley Graham, whom he had married in 1951, a year after Nina's death, wondered that a man should be laurelled and lionized around the world and yet forbidden to enter the Harvard Club back home. By 1960, he was able to accept Nkrumah's invitation to come to Ghana and celebrate the final constitutional separation from Britain, as Ghana became a Republic. He also made a visit to Lagos, where he met Tom Mboya, the Kenyan independence leader and, as it happens, a friend and mentor of Barack Obama, Sr.[24] A year later, in 1961, Du Bois moved to Ghana for good . . . and finally joined the Communist Party. In 1963, the boy from Great Barrington, Massachusetts, denied a new U.S. passport by the American Embassy in Accra, became a citizen of that African nation. He was ninety-five.

This was the man who wrote *The Souls of Black Folk*. And what a paradoxical figure he is. He was a man of the left, but also an elitist and a dandy, who developed the notion that the African-American community should be led by what he called a "Talented Tenth."[25] He could be bitterly anticlerical, and yet his works are etched by the Christian narrative of suffering and redemption. He was profoundly committed to literature, poetry, art, and music, writing movingly of coming to know Beethoven and Wagner, Titian and Rembrandt when he traveled to Europe. He declared that "art is not simply works of art; it is the spirit that knows Beauty, that has music in its soul and the color of sunsets in its headkerchiefs; that can dance on a flaming world and make the world dance, too."[26] But he also announced, "all art is propaganda and ever must be, despite the wailing of purists."[27] He wrote that his people were "Americans, not only by birth and by citizenship, but by our political ideals, our language, our religion"; but he claimed membership, too, in a black race that transcended nationalities. And, in the end, his love of race and disappointment with America led him to renounce his American citizenship and take up with the new nation of Ghana.

Du Bois's adoption of a homeland on the African continent did not reflect a loss of interest in the fate of the Negro in America. Among his last acts was to compose a telegram of support on August 27, 1963, to the March on Washington—a message that went out before he went to sleep on the night he died, five years short of a century old. Roy Wilkins announced his death to the vast crowds gathered on the Washington Mall. "If you want to read something that applies to 1963," Wilkins told them, "go back and get a volume of *The Souls of Black Folk* by Du Bois published in 1903." Du Bois's state funeral in Accra, the next day, was one of the first great public events in the post-Independence history of Ghana: President Nkrumah hailed him as "a real friend and father to me."[28] No one came from the United States Embassy to represent the country of his birth. If he died angry at America, he had his reasons.

Of course, indignation was one of his modes. He had raged at America, off and on, for much of his life, so that was nothing new. Yet his feelings were anything but unalloyed. In his posthumously published memoir, he invokes "that dichotomy which all my life has characterized my thought: how far can love for my oppressed race accord with love for the oppressing country? And when these loyalties diverge, where shall my soul find refuge?"[29] What's clear is that, right to his Ghanaian end, his identity was intimately tied up with his Americanness; and if his American nationalism was that of the patriot betrayed, pained by the inability of his country to live up to her best self, well, those sentiments are sentiments you can only have *as* an American. When the decision in *Brown v. Board of Education* was announced, Du Bois said, famously: "I have seen the impossible happen."[30] (Many people, I am sure, had the same thought when another American son of Africa was elected to the Presidency half a century later.) Did Du Bois ever give up on this country of ours, which he once called, only half in irony, "knightly America"? Or did he see in the growing successes of Dr. King and the Civil Rights movement the possibility of a future in which a thoughtful and self-respecting black man could love America without reservation?

Du Bois was America's last romantic. And romantic love, in the tradition established by the troubadours, is always an impossible love. It admits impediment, even as it strives to overcome impediment. So it was with Du Bois's arguments over the Negro's definition and destiny. Du Bois's arguments were tethered to the varieties of racial romanticism and postromantic thought that he took from Germany's intellectual traditions; they were kin to the ideas through which Germany sought to define itself as a nation among nations. But these arguments mattered, he believed, to the fate of humanity in general, not just to black people in particular. They mattered to him, above all, because at their heart were puzzles about who he was himself, that brilliant son of Great Barrington. He faced in a peculiarly public way one question that faces every human being: What am I to do with the identities that fate has given me? In exploring his answers, and the life they enabled him to make, we can learn something about how to shape our own—no doubt, different—responses.

CHAPTER ONE

The Awakening

> It was in Germany that my first
> awakening to social reform began.
> —W. E. B. Du Bois, "An Appreciation"

Du Bois boarded the Dutch steamship *Amsterdam* and set sail for Europe in July of 1892. On the first of August, a couple of weeks later, he disembarked in Rotterdam. Soon he was on a steamer, making his way along the Rhine. His academic semester did not start until late October and he was in no rush. He visited Düsseldorf, Cologne, and Frankfurt. In Eisenach, the birthplace of Bach and the site of the Schloss Wartburg, where Luther had translated the Bible into German, he lived in rooms let by the pastor of the local church, Johannes Marbach, and brushed up his German.[1] He picnicked with the Marbach family, went to a ball with their daughter, Dora, and ruefully demurred when she brought up the subject of marriage. ("Es war' so schön gewesen/Es hätt' nicht sollen sein," he wrote years later. "It would have been so lovely/It was not meant to be."[2]) Then, after a trip that took him through Weimar and Leipzig, he arrived at Berlin in mid-October, where he was warmly welcomed by the Rector, Rudolph Virchow, and promptly enrolled in five lecture courses and a seminar.[3]

The University of Berlin was then the largest university in the Zweites Reich, at the apex of a German academic system that had re-created the university by inventing modern graduate education. Still, Du Bois—with his pair of BAs and two years of graduate studies at Harvard—was scarcely unformed when he arrived. During his Cambridge years, Albert Bushnell Hart had trained him in history; Frank Taussig taught him Ricardian economics; George Santayana, just four years his senior, taught him Hegel and Kant. William James had taken a particular interest in him, entertaining him at home as well as teaching him ethics. As a member of Harvard's Philosophical Club, Du Bois also had wide-ranging conversations with two leading lights of American Hegelianism, George Herbert Palmer, who chaired the philosophy department, and Josiah Royce, Du Bois's old forensics instructor. But all of them had studied in Germany; Santayana,

Hart, and Taussig had trained at the University of Berlin. A German degree was the ironclad credential, and Du Bois was determined that it would be his. Not that it was merely a matter of credentialism. To the surging Berlin Spree, Cambridge's Charles River could seem, intellectually speaking, a mere side-channel. Du Bois wanted to visit the source.

What he couldn't have anticipated is that he would fall in love—not just with Dora but with her country. Du Bois wrote of how he "thrilled at the sight" of the Emperor Wilhelm II parading on horseback along Unter den Linden and through the Brandenburg Gate. Afterward, he wrote, "I even trimmed my beard and mustache to a fashion like his," a practice he maintained for the rest of his life.[4] His Wilhelmine affections would always stare at him in the mirror. His decision to marry, a few years later, was itself infused with the love he had for Germany: Nina Gomer's mother was a German, from Alsace, and, writing in *Darkwater,* he describes his bride not just as "a slip of a girl, beautifully dark-eyed" but as "thorough and good as a German housewife."[5]

The reason for his devotion went beyond his love for German music, poetry, and art. Germany was the first place where Du Bois experienced life without the daily cruelties and public insults of racism. "In the days of my Sturm und Drang," he wrote, "this was the land where I first met white folk who treated me as a human being."[6] And, in turn, the Negro came to see white folks beyond the prism of race: "I met men and women as I had never met them before. Slowly they became, not white folks but folks."[7] The sense of personal liberation he felt cannot be overestimated. "I became more human; learned the place in life of 'Wine, Women, and Song'; I ceased to hate or suspect people simply because they belonged to one race or color," he recalled. What mattered more than his complexion was that he had acquired the silk tie, gloves, and walking stick that marked him as a member of the *Bildungsbürgertum* (that splendid German expression for the educated bourgeoisie). To the typical Berliner, as Du Bois understood, he was not a member of a subordinate American caste; he was, however exotic his hue, "just a man of the somewhat privileged student rank, with whom they were glad to meet and talk over the world."[8]

I became more human—it is a powerful tribute. Did he mean that he felt liberated, in a sense, from his race? Du Bois, in the autobiographical passages he wrote and rewrote throughout his life, was alert to that suspicion, for he was at pains to insist otherwise: "The unity beneath all life clutched me. I was not less fanatically a Negro, but 'Negro' meant a greater, broader sense of humanity and world-fellowship. I felt myself standing, not against the world, but simply against American narrowness and color prejudice, with the greater, finer world at my back urging me on."[9]

The Scholar and the State

Urging him on—to what? One thing that would have impressed Du Bois, even outside of the classrooms, was the model of real-world engagement that the Berlin faculty represented. Unter den Linden 6 was no ivory tower. Most of the professors whose classes he attended in his first semester had political careers. The political economist Adolf Wagner, with whom Du Bois worked closely, was an early member of the Christian Social Party, had served as a policy advisor to Chancellors Otto von Bismarck and Leo von Caprivi, and had been a member of the Prussian house of representatives; Rudolf Gneist, whose course on Prussian state reforms Du Bois took, was a member of the Prussian Council of State.[10] Heinrich von Treitschke, whose lecture course on Prussian political history Du Bois attended, and who was, the young student decided, "by far the most interesting of the professors . . . the German Machiavelli," served in the Reichstag, the Imperial Diet.[11]

In their scholarly work, too, many of Du Bois's professors grappled with the inequality of wealth and power, and its political consequences. Gneist worried that "the dependence of the needy on the affluent . . . curtails freedom in the State, bringing about that everlasting conflict of interests, which strive, on the one hand, to strengthen, on the other to relax or remove the shackles of thralldom." For the neo-Rankean Max Lenz, with whom Du Bois took three courses, there was a political tension between the liberal state and the autonomy of the individual conscience—one that could be traced to the Reformation and had yet to be resolved. Du Bois's statistics professor, August Meitzen (the mentor of Max Weber), was the author of an 1876 work entitled "The Joint Responsibility of The Educated and Propertied Classes for the Welfare of the Working Classes."[12]

Then there was Gustav von Schmoller, whose seminar Du Bois took, and with whom Du Bois did a course of independent research. The no-longer-young luminary of the Younger Historical School of

Economics—"A large man of about 50 with flowing
beard, grown bald and prematurely gray," was how
Du Bois described him at the time[13]—Schmoller
served, like Gneist, in the Prussian Council of State.
But he was more influential as a founder, along with
Wagner, of the Verein für Sozialpolitik, the Association for Social Policy. Wagner and Schmoller—
branded *"Kathedersozialisten,"* lectern-socialists, by
the likes of Treitschke—explicitly hoped that their
scholarship would influence the administration of
the Reich.[14] Scholarship, in Schmoller's view, could be
both dispassionate and engaged. Du Bois recorded
one of his teacher's aphorisms in his notebook: "My
school tries as far as possible to leave the *sollen* for a
later stage and study the *geschehen* as other sciences
have done." Schmoller wasn't untheoretical; he was,
for one thing, a careful reader of William Whewell
on induction. What he insisted on was simply that
your conclusions flow from your observations; you
could infer patterns, even (specific and situated) rules,
by sifting through the data. But inferring the rule
was what you had to do; you couldn't plant it there
yourself, like a corrupt police officer dumping a drop
gun. Nor could you derive economic truths from a

priori first principles, as did Carl Menger and others of what the Prussian historical economists called "the Austrian school."[15]

But leaving the sollen for a later stage did not mean leaving the sollen to wither on the vine. Schmoller—who praised Bismarck's social reforms, such as compulsory health insurance for workers, as the sort of meliorism that justice and social stability required—thought that the government "had a moral duty to alleviate undue hardships."[16] The scholar would make the close and careful observations; then he would be able to infer historical patterns that could help guide the policy makers.

Wagner, who was also identified with the Historical School, held that the "higher classes" and the state were obliged to recognize "the just kernel contained in the socialistic demands." He denied that he was a spokesman for the socialists, and, indeed, his aims were the opposite of revolutionary. Nevertheless, he thought policy should aim, as far as possible, to reduce the "evil that grows out of this fact and to keep the existing inequalities from increasing. We have the means of doing this in progressive measure. If we use these means, we have then performed our duties, and this may be demanded of us; no more, but also not less."[17] Noblesse oblige.

And so the Historical School represented a union between political engagement and a just-the-facts approach to social and economic history. Schmoller and other members of the Verein didn't think that the ethical could be excluded from historical studies, not least because the development of the ethical was itself a historical phenomenon. Indeed, given that our ethical forces, our sittliche Kräfte, took shape within traditions and institutions, the reform of such things would elevate our moral character. (In this sense, the German economist Samuel Paul Altmann wrote in 1904, Schmoller's "system of ethics aspires to a reconciliation of individualistic and collectivistic theories.")[18]

This conception of the social sciences as, at core, ethical, is why Schmoller could alternate dreary enumerations with heated, almost prophetic warnings. He inveighed against the growing economic inequalities, the spread of "morally reprehensible forms of trade," the mismatch between income and accomplishment, warning that they would drive a "nail in the coffin of any existing system of property."[19] Still, his fundamental picture was one in which class conflict was the inevitable consequence of the division of labor in society. The gradual improvements in social organization, from the Greek city-state through the Roman republic and the Middle Ages, down to the present were, he wrote, "steps on the hard and thorny path to a greater, more stable regime without too much class abuse."[20] "'Too much" class abuse, he thought, produced the revolts and revolutions he cataloged in his historical survey of the division of labor.

Class struggle was the result of class domination; and class domination, which could be seen again and again in the historical archive, meant that the stronger classes used the state to take advantage of the weaker classes.[21] So some "class abuse" was inevitable. Nevertheless, all the classes in a single society had not only opposed economic interests but also spiritual *(geistige)* interests in common.[22] Especially in a nation of men and women of common origins, a single stock, the shared interests could mitigate the abuses in the name of the opposed ones. Schmoller presented these claims as discoveries of historical analysis, not as deductions from a picture of human nature. His voluminous studies are filled with the sort of learned references to the human past that we recall from reading Max Weber.

Du Bois was mindful of Schmoller's epistemic hygiene when he warned, in *The Philadelphia Negro,*

> The best available methods of sociological research are at present so liable to inaccuracies that the careful student discloses the results of individual research with diffidence; he knows that they are liable to error from the seemingly ineradicable faults of the statistical method, to even greater error from the methods of general observation, and, above all, he must ever tremble lest some personal bias, some moral conviction or some unconscious trend of thought due to previous training, has to a degree distorted the picture in his view. Convictions on all great matters of human interest one must have to a greater or less degree, and they will enter to some extent into the most cold-blooded of scientific research as a disturbing factor.[23]

Note that we aren't to disapprove of moral conviction as such; it's only where it threatens to "distort the picture" that we must rein it in. But he isn't departing from this model when, in the same study, he moves beyond methodological cautions, tables, charts, and statistical summaries to announce the true significance of the Negro Problem:

The battle involves more than a mere altruistic interest in an alien people. It is a battle for humanity and human culture. If in the hey-dey of the greatest of the world's civilizations, it is possible for one people ruthlessly to steal another, drag them helpless across the water, enslave them, debauch them, and then slowly murder them by economic and social exclusion until they disappear from the face of the earth—if the consummation of such a crime be possible in the twentieth century, then our civilization is vain and the republic is a mockery and a farce.[24]

And Du Bois would have found more than methodological and moral points of affinity with the historical school. A central concern of the historical economists was with the "Social Question," *die Soziale Frage*—the set of problems entrained by industrialization, as agrarian workers became industrial labor and a new underclass came into existence. Might not the social question provide a model for how the *Negerfrage* might be conceived?[25] The possible parallels would not have been lost on the Germans. Schmoller says, in passing, in his book on the social question, that class conflict can be amplified when class difference and race difference coexist, where a "higher race" subjects other "racial elements."[26] (Du Bois's Berlin teachers were not unaware of his race: he later conjectured that his "unusual coloring and so forth" might have helped him gain entrance to the oversubscribed seminars of Wagner and Schmoller.)[27] The affinities of the social and the Negro questions would have been evident to all.

The Contest of Faculties

Du Bois became a member of the Verein in 1893. In so doing, he had joined a side in a battle that, despite a temporary lull, was far from over. He arrived in the aftermath of a fierce *Methodenstreit,* a conflict over methods. Schmoller, known as the "professor-maker" for his success in placing his protégés, had spent a fair amount of the previous decade defending the historical school against Carl Menger and the other insurgents of what Schmoller contemptuously dubbed "the Austrian school" of economics, one of the forerunners of modern neoclassical economics. As is the way with academic disputation, the tendency was to distort the opponent's doctrines—and clarify one's own.

Du Bois, a young man who planned to "study scientifically the Negro question past and present, with a view to its best solution," as he promised the Slater Fund, knew that the stakes were real.[28] The scholar Axel Schäfer pithily observes that the historical school "reflected Hegelian metaphysics, Kantian epistemology, and Herderian historicism."[29] This was a not-entirely-harmonious combination of impulses; but neither, apparently, were they wholly incompatible. Historicism, of this sort, set itself against eternal laws. It was attuned, rather, to the contingent and provisional nature of our cultural and social inheritances. Ethical systems weren't baked into some transcendent feature of humanity; they emerged, and unfolded, through social activity, through the shifting internal structures of society. The economic organization of a society, for Schmoller, didn't reflect timeless natural laws—*pace* the Austrians—but arose from the ethical views of various economic actors (the family, the community, the firm, and the state), views that were themselves the product of social and historical forces.

It isn't that the historical economists were skeptical of progress. Schmoller believed that, as he wrote, "an ever growing share of the population partaking of the higher goods of culture, Bildung and wealth," was a "great general goal of world history."[30] But progress would arise from human strivings, by the enlistment of our moral energies. Timeless laws wouldn't do the work for us. Accordingly, he scoffed at the notion that nonintervention, laissez-faire, would allow some natural, ideal equilibrium to establish itself. He had no patience for an economic dogma that took individualism to be an ideal and "considered the state to be almost unnecessary and politicians to be scoundrels." The model of *homo economicus*—"die Theorie der natürlichen Volkswirtschaft" (the theory of the natural economy)—was "in toto, based on an incomplete analysis of man."[31] Society was not merely an assemblage of rational individuals; it was also something like an organism, which could be guided wisely or unwisely, and the efforts of prudent governance were indispensable to creating a more just social order.[32] Still, Schmoller, like Wagner, saw error in either direction. The atomistic individualism of the despised Manchester School was to be shunned. But so was the liberty-denying organicism of the old conservatives down the hall, not to mention the new revolutionaries on the streets outside.

An up-and-coming theorist of race would have been attracted to Schmoller's resistance to methodological individualism, not just to his powerful melding—in both theory and practice—of social reform and

empirical scholarship. The school's inveterate suspicion toward anything that boasted of being "natürlich"
was a valuable precaution, too. And yet a historical
study of the historical school would have noted certain perplexities. Apparently it was too much to ask
that, say, racial explanations of historical events, especially those offered with a Social Darwinian tilt, would
be among the things to be historicized—taken as an
explanandum rather than an explanans. You might
have thought that Herbert Spenser's doctrines had a
Manchesterian accent. But Adolph Wagner was con-
vinced, for instance, that "the Gallic race, or the present French hybrid of which the Gauls still form the
chief part, is threatened more and more with suppression by Germanthum. In the end there awaits it
the fate of all lower organisms in the Darwinian
struggle for existence."[33] Nor did theoretical caution
dampen the Verein members' ardor for colonialism.
At one Verein meeting, Max Weber warned of the
dangers of bringing in Polish workers, who might in-
terbreed with the natives; possibly Chinese coolies
would be safer, because less likely to sully the stock.[34]

But then Du Bois could have no illusions that either the Verein or the Kaiserreich itself was free of
prejudice and discrimination. He was particularly

struck by the antagonism between Poles and Germans, and the prevalence of anti-Semitism did not pass him by either. He admired the rector of the university, Virchow, who was a leading light in progressive politics within the Reichstag and a foe of bigotry. ("If different races would recognize one another as independent co-laborers in the great field of humanity, if all possessed a modesty which would allow them to see merits in neighboring people, much of the strife now agitating the world would disappear," Virchow avowed.)[35] Yet Virchow had to contend with dark accusations that he was *judenfreundlich,* philosemitic. Treitschke once startled Du Bois by bursting out with a statement about the inferiority of the mulatto. ("Die Mulatten sind niedrig! Sie fühlen sich niedrig": Mulattoes are inferior! They feel themselves inferior.) But Du Bois was sure that Treitschke hadn't even noticed his presence in the crowded lecture hall. There was plenty of race prejudice about, but, for a change, it wasn't personally directed toward him.[36]

Treitschke was an outspoken antagonist of Schmoller and Wagner's when it came to political reform; their debates form another Methodenstreit of sorts. Yet he was a figure of particular fascination for Du Bois. When he describes Treitschke's sudden outburst about "die Mulatten," it is alongside a list of the professor's other comic eccentricities. Du Bois's admiration for the historian is undimmed: "Yet von Treitschke was not a narrow man," he asserts.[37] Certainly the historian's hostility to egalitarianism—"nature forms all her higher creatures unequally," he thought—was not foreign to the young Du Bois. ("In many respects it is right and proper to judge a people by its best classes," he wrote in *The Philadelphia Negro*. After all, "the highest class of any group represents its possibilities rather than its exceptions, as is so often assumed in regard to the Negro."[38]) More than that, he seems to have seen thrilling possibilities in the historian's racial romanticism. Du Bois, that is, was drawn to him not despite his grand conception of race and culture as a motive force in history but because of it.

"Man alone is an historical existence, and hence the one true societary being," Treitschke wrote. (This was in the course of debating Schmoller but it was a recurrent motif in his thought.)

He receives in language and morality, in law and industry, the works of the fathers. They live with him and he is effective by means of them. He stands as a living, and if he wills, a conscious link in the chain of times. . . . He lives only in and through submitting himself to the aggregate culture of his people.[39]

If Du Bois kindled to the "fire-eating Pan-German," it was because this conception of culture had a potent allure for him. The challenge was to take its power without its parochialism—to steal the fire without getting burned.

CHAPTER TWO

Culture and Cosmopolitanism

> Two souls, alas, are dwelling in my breast,
> And one desires to break off from the other.
> —Johann Wolfgang von Goethe, *Faust*

THE notion of culture Du Bois encountered in Berlin had deep roots . . . and glossy foilage. One useful point of entry to the conceptual world the young scholar found in Berlin is in the work of Johann Gottfried Herder, the great German nationalist and philosopher of romanticism. Du Bois absorbed not only Herder's romantic conception of individuality but also the Herderian picture of the spiritual life of nations. For Herder, writing before the ascendancy of the modern nation-state, each nation has a distinct governing spirit, its *Volksgeist* (a word one might translate as "national soul"), which is expressed in every aspect of its social and cultural life. So the character of a nation can be found not only in the writings of its literary geniuses—in Goethe and Hölderlin—but also in its folklore; for example, the folk songs and the folk tales collected, under Herder's inspiration, by Jacob and Wilhelm Grimm.[1]

For Herder, as for Du Bois, each Volksgeist possesses something of distinctive value. One of Herder's claims about historical method is that we must recognize how different the inner life of different peoples is. (Raymond Williams thought that Herder was the first writer to use "culture" in the plural.)[2] Nevertheless, Herder maintained with equal fervor that "Human kind is a single thing, a whole: we work and suffer, sow and reap for each other."[3] Indeed part of the providential point of human history is that each people, each Volk, should express its distinct character through its history, because it is only through each nation's following its distinctive path that history as a whole can achieve its meaning.

Du Bois's debt to this intellectual legacy—the theory of the Volksgeist—is hard to avoid: it hovers over the title of his best-known book. He is showing his readers the *Geister* (this is the plural of *Geist*) of a black Volk. The Herderian tendency is present as well in Du Bois's citations in *The Souls of Black Folk,* not only of German high culture but also of its folk culture, as

when he quotes a German folk song in the final pages:
"Jetz Geh i' an's brunele, trink' aber net." (One might
translate this as: "Now I's goin' to de well, but ain't
gonna drink.")[4] In the final chapter of that book, Du
Bois argues that the black soul is to be found most
perfectly expressed in the spirituals. This attention
to the folk-culture of a people had, as I say, been central to the first flush of romantic nationalism. Herder
would have understood exactly why Du Bois pref-
aced each chapter of *Souls* with both a literary epigraph and a phrase of a Negro spiritual (though,
with his usual sense for a distinctive formulation, Du
Bois called the spirituals the "Sorrow Songs"). Negro
spirituals were the folksong, the *Volksdichtung,* of
Afro-America.

Indeed, the Herderian strain in Du Bois's cultural cosmopolitanism fairly courses through *Souls.*
It's in his openness to the achievements of other
civilizations—his celebration of European culture,
high and low. Recall those well-known lines from the
book:

I sit with Shakespeare and he winces not. Across
the color line I move arm in arm with Balzac and
Dumas, where smiling men and welcoming women

glide in gilded halls. From out the caves of evening that swing between the strong-limbed earth and the tracery of the stars, I summon Aristotle and Aurelius and what soul I will, and they come all graciously with no scorn nor condescension. So, wed with Truth, I dwell above the Veil.[5]

We can hear Herder, too, in the Wagnerian Schwär-merei suffusing the chapter "Of the Coming of John," a story of two Johns, one black and one white, who are playmates as children but set on a fatal collision course as men. At one point, the black John is moved beyond measure by Wagner's music: "He sat in dreamland, and started when, after a hush, rose high and clear the music of Lohengrin's swan. The infinite beauty of the wail lingered and swept through every muscle of his frame, and put it all a-tune."[6]

Russell Berman has imaginatively traced links be-tween the "Lohengrin" story and the story in "Of the Coming of John." Yet there may be echoes down the ages, too, of Herder's poem "Die Brüder," about a black boy and a white boy who have been raised together— Milchbrüder (foster brothers), of course, not Blut-brüder (blood brothers)—and whose fraternity is un-done when the white brother, grown to manhood, proves to be another "white devil" and turns on his black brother.[7] The poem is one of Herder's Neger-Idyllen (Negro Idylls), and they have a decisively anti-slavery (and anticolonial) tone.

Here we approach the other dimension of Herder's cosmopolitanism, the moral dimension, and, again, it is a point of affinity with Du Bois. Herder's historicism could, it's true, be mistaken as relativist. "One observes that propositions for which at certain times each person would have sacrificed his last drop of blood at other times get damned to the fire by precisely the same nation," he observed.[8] Certainly, Herder believed that people and societies were always changing: "one needs a magic mirror" to recognize the same creature among the different forms it takes over time, so much does time change things.[9] But what looks like relativism was wielded in the cause of a universal humanism; it was an invitation to interrogate our own ethnocentrism. He supposed, for instance, that

the negro has as much right to term his savage robbers albinoes and white devils, degenerated through the weakness of nature, as we have to deem him the emblem of evil, and a descendant of Ham, branded by his father's curse. I, might he say, I the black, am the original man. I have taken the deepest draughts from the source of life, the Sun: on me, and on every thing around me, it has acted with the greatest energy and vivacity. Behold my country. . . . Here each element swarms with life, and I am the centre of this vital action.[10]

He wrote, as in the Neger-Idyllen, with resolute horror about slavery and colonial exploitation.[11]

Herder's emphasis on the cultural inheritances of peoples—the Nationaldichtkunst (National Poetic Art), the Nationalschatz (National Treasure), and so on—and his belief that each group "has the center of its happiness *within itself*" was disciplined by his notion of *Humanität*. It was a notion he struggled to pin down, but conceived in terms of "Vernunft und Billigkeit"—reason and equity—and it could be kindled with the "edles Feuer des Mitgefühls," the noble fire of sympathy.[12]

To say that Du Bois was a cosmopolitan nationalist may sound, to contemporary readers, like an oxymoron, a matter, at the very least, of two contending souls. Surely cosmopolitanism—the idea that all human beings are, in some sense, fellow citizens of the

world—is necessarily the opposite of nationalism—
the conviction that the boundaries of nationality
should be the boundaries of citizenship? Our brief
reading of Herder shows that this is not an assumption that someone with Du Bois's intellectual back-
ground would have made. "Cosmopolitanism and nationalism stood side by side in a close, living relationship
for a long time,"[13] wrote the historian Friedrich Meinecke, who, during Du Bois's Berlin days, worked at
the Prussian State Archives a few blocks away, having
graduated from the university only a few years earlier. Here, in a study that appeared just a few years
after *Souls* was published, Meinecke was discussing
Johann Gottlieb Fichte, who had been a philosopher
at the University of Berlin and was a key figure in the
transition from Kant to Hegel; but the point he is
making applies quite widely. (The book in which he
makes it is titled *Weltbürgertum und Nationalstaat:
Studien zur Genesis des deutschen Nationalstaats—
Cosmopolitanism and the National State: Studies in the
Genesis of the German National State.*) Cosmopolitanism and nationalism were the warp and weft of much
nineteenth-century liberal thought: the great Italian
Patriot Giuseppe Mazzini was quite clear that a devotion to one's country was a the god-given vehicle to

enable us to advance "the moral improvement and progress of Humanity," rather as Burke had supposed that to "love the little platoon we belong to in society" was the first link in a series that would lead us to the love of mankind.[14] In a similar cadence, Du Bois would argue, in 1897, that "The race idea, the race spirit, the race ideal" is "the vastest and most ingenious invention for human progress."[15]

In Du Bois's Berlin, to be sure, not a few were determined to put asunder what the cosmopolitan theorists of the nation had joined together. There was Treitschke, of course, with his notions of separate and unequal racial destinies. Adolf Wagner, too, had inveighed, in an 1870 pamphlet, against cosmopolitan tendencies:

> O Germany, when will your own sons stop wounding you to the point of death with their fanatical objectivity? When, finally, will a healthy national egotism, beside all this protecting of the rights of others, think first of the wellbeing of its own state and abandon the disastrous cosmopolitanism with which we protect the warranted and unwarranted sensitivities of foreign countries?

Meinecke himself, having so carefully documented the cosmopolitan patriotism of Schiller, Schlegel, Fichte, and the rest, regarded the turn away from it as a positive development, which made possible the establishment of a proper German nation-state—the merging of Machtstaat and Kulturstaat, uniting the political with the cultural nation.[16]

So we shouldn't imagine that cosmopolitanism was simply parading happily along Unter den Linden on a prancing charger. It faced serious and sophisticated challenges, not least from new ideologies of nationalism. But the forms of German nationalism that were abandoning their cosmopolitan attachments—with what, in retrospect, are bound to seem disastrous results—simply couldn't perform the task that Du Bois considered critical. He had no use for a nationalism that made claims only upon its own nationals; this was a nationalism of already established might. He had to make claims upon humanity. Nationalists before the ascendancy of the nation-state recognized that the demand for national rights made sense as a moral demand only if it was claimed equally for all nations. The strategy of the argument is one that Kant made familiar. My dignity cannot matter because it is mine; it has to matter because it is dignity. And if it is dignity that matters, then your dignity matters to. So, too, *mutatis mutandis,* for nationality. In Du Bois's view, the Negro legitimately had a higher degree of concern for his own kind, but this view was framed within the recognition both that they had obligations to people of other races and that they would gain greatly from conversation across the races. Still, "the race spirit" could not advance itself without much individual and collective striving. The notion of striving is, indeed, *required* if we are to grasp more fully the entailments of this "spirit."

Spiritual Strivings

Consider the essay in *Souls* that Du Bois called "Of Our Spiritual Strivings" (adapted from his 1897 *Atlantic* article, "Strivings of the Negro People"). The German word for striving is *streben*. In the later eighteenth century, Fichte had taken that word, which occurs often in the writings of Lutheran Pietists (who were constantly, well, striving for holiness and toward God), and made it one of the key technical ideas of his development of Kantian philosophy. Striving is Fichte's term for human action, the process in which the self overcomes the resistance of the external world; or, as he puts it, the I acts on a resistant not-I *(nicht-Ich)*. Given the intellectual world he inhabited—he conversed with Friedrich Schiller and Wilhelm von Humboldt, both of whom he knew when he had his first chair of philosophy in Jena (he later took a chair at the University of Berlin); and the works of Goethe and Herder were always near at hand—we wouldn't want to suggest the romantic taste for the idea of striving derives from him alone. But streben, like Geist, is a word that had both a wide circulation and narrower technical uses. Someone who was, like Du Bois, an heir to this intellectual history must have taken up these concepts with a sense of their philosophical weight.

Striving is everywhere in the literature of romanticism; in the prologue to Faust, Goethe's God tells Mephistopheles: "Es irrt der Mensch so lang er strebt." "Man errs so long as he strives"; and so, as long as we are on earth, we human beings are erring and striving. (In a passage that more clearly impressed Du Bois, Faust later lamented of the two souls contending within his breast: "Zwei Seelen wohnen, ach! in meiner Brust,/Die eine will sich von der andern trennen"—Two souls, alas, are dwelling in my breast,/

And one desires to break off from the other.) But striving is central in late romanticism, too, as when Rilke wrote these famous words in 1898:

> Niemals bin ich allein.
> Viele, die vor mir lebten
> und fort von mir strebten,
> webten,
> webten
> an meinem Sein.[17]

The idea of life as a striving for the infinite, a search to transcend the inevitable resistance of the world, appealed to the spirit of romanticism that developed as the first great cultural reaction to the Enlightenment, a movement in which Fichte, the philosopher, and Goethe, the poet and savant, were central.[18] So, too, did the yearning for wholeness, for the project of bringing the superficially conflicting elements of reality into a unity; a project whose completion is, of course, forever beyond our grasp. For romanticism, striving's aim was a pleasingly unreachable wholeness.

Let's explore, then, the possibility that the language of souls striving—which might seem to us merely casually metaphorical or conventionally pious—actually trails a philosophical theory. We can return, for the moment, to Du Bois's frequent use of the word "soul" and take seriously the idea that it really means "Geist"; that, in some sense to be specified, our topic is *geistige Streben*.

The word "Geist" has a wider range of meaning than any of the English words we might use to translate it. In particular, it can mean soul, spirit, or mind. Another sense, which we can largely ignore, is shared with English in our word "ghost," which now only has the sense of "spirit" when it is used to refer to the Holy Ghost. But this particular religious resonance should remind us that the words "soul" and "spirit," which Du Bois uses often, have, for us, a strongly religious quality. While there is no doubt that Hegel's philosophical use of "Geist" was borrowed and developed from its earlier Christian uses, it acquired a more purely philosophical sense when it became the key concept of his metaphysics. Hegel's *Phänomenologie des Geistes* has been translated both as *The Phenomenology of Spirit* and as *The Phenomenology of Mind;* but however you translate "Geist," its meaning had diverged far from the Christian idea of the soul, which came to repose in the term *Seele*. As a result, an educated German reader need hear nothing specifically religious in talk of the Geist.

So put aside for the moment the religious reso-
nances of "soul," take seriously the thought that striving is what souls do, and read again this well-thumbed
passage, from "Of Our Spiritual Strivings":

> It is a peculiar sensation, this double-consciousness,
> this sense of always looking at one's self through
> the eyes of others, of measuring one's soul by the
> tape of a world that looks on in amused contempt
> and pity. One ever feels his two-ness,—an Ameri-
> can, a Negro; two souls, two thoughts, two unrec-
> onciled strivings; two warring ideals in one dark
> body, whose dogged strength alone keeps it from
> being torn asunder.[19]

Once we take these references to souls as an invo-
cation of a theoretical idea, the difficulty for this interpretation is straightforward enough: How can a
person have more than one soul? We have assembled
the materials for an answer. We can think of the soul
here not as an individual's unique possession, but
rather as something she shares with the folk to which
she belongs: think of it, that is, as a Volksgeist. Think
of each Volksgeist, too, as striving to realize itself
against a resisting not-I. Then a person who belongs
to more than one people could share in two souls,

each defined, in part, by its striving against a world that contains other souls. Furthermore, as Du Bois requires, a person who had both a Negro and an American soul could participate in the intellectual and cultural—the geistige—life of both, and thus see herself through both a Negro and an American lens. Because the two visions are at odds, this person would, indeed, have two warring ideals contending within a single body. In describing this putative affliction, Du Bois was, in effect, rejecting the notion that each of us could participate in only one Volksgeist; an individual person could be, in part, the product of the souls of the various folks to which she belonged. (This is perhaps the possibility that horrified Treitschke when he spoke of the mulatto!)

In the passage immediately following the one we have been discussing, Du Bois argues that "the history of the American Negro is the history of this strife,—this longing to attain self-conscious manhood, to merge his double self into a better and truer self." And he goes on to gesture toward a vaguely Fichtean synthesis:

> In this merging he wishes neither of the older selves to be lost. He would not Africanize America, for

America has too much to teach the world and Africa. He would not bleach his Negro soul in a flood of white Americanism, for he knows that Negro blood has a message for the world. He simply wishes to make it possible for a man to be both a Negro and an American, without being cursed and spit upon by his fellows, without having the doors of Opportunity closed roughly in his face.[20]

If to have a Negro soul just *is* to participate in the collective life of the Negro folk, then there is nothing to stop you having an American soul because you participate in the collective life of an American folk as well. And the idea can be generalized. For a folk is just a people—a historically enduring procession of somehow-connected individuals. And while nations and races, as Du Bois's contemporaries conceived of them, provided examples of such collections, it may be open to you to extend the idea to other kinds of people. In fact, any group might have a soul, if a soul is just defined as a common principle that binds the group together, the thing whose sharing makes them one. We could, in theory, speak of the disparate souls that women or Baptists or lesbians or philologists share. Hegel wrote, "Der Geist ist das sittliche Leben eines Volks." (The spirit is the ethical life—the shared traditions of behavior—of a people.)[21] Perhaps Du Bois meant us to take this idea seriously. We could, then, develop in this language an account of what it is to be a human being with multiple souls, or selves, or, as we might now say, identities. I'll return to this thought later. For now, let me just note one more consequence of that placing of the Negro as a Folk among Folks: it presupposes a reference to a global perspective, the perspective of humanity.[22] Black Folk must find their place among the nations; that they *have* a place is what we might call Herder's axiom. Du Bois is a cosmopolitan through and through.

The Color Line

Probably the most often-quoted line in *The Souls of Black Folk* appears twice in that book: "The problem of the twentieth century is the problem of the color-line." Du Bois first offered this formulation in his speech "To the Nations of the World" at the first Pan-African Conference, organized by the Trinidadian Henry Sylvester Williams in London in 1900. In the course of discussing the exploitation of the nonwhite world by European empires, Du Bois had said this:

The problem of the twentieth century is the problem of the color-line, the question as to how far differences of race—which show themselves chiefly in the color of the skin and the texture of the hair—will hereafter be made the basis of denying to over half the world the right of sharing to their utmost ability the opportunities and privileges of modern civilization. . . .

In any case, the modern world must remember that in this age, when the ends of the world are being brought so near together, the millions of black men in Africa, America and the Islands of the Sea, not to speak of the brown and yellow myriads elsewhere, are bound to have a great influence upon the world in the future, by reason of sheer numbers and physical contact. If now the world of culture bends itself towards giving Negroes and other dark men the largest and broadest opportunity for education and self-development, then this contact and influence is bound to have a beneficial effect upon the world and hasten progress. But if, by reason of carelessness, prejudice, greed and injustice, the black world is to be exploited and ravished and degraded, the results must be deplorable, if not fatal—not simply to them, but to the high ideals of justice, freedom and culture which a thousand years of Christian civilization have held before Europe.[23]

In *Souls,* too, the "color-line" is a matter of "the relation of the darker to the lighter races of men in Asia and Africa, in America and the islands of the sea."[24] Again, Du Bois's tendency to go global is striking. *Souls* is about black life in America, but notice that Du Bois prefaces this discussion of Reconstruction in the American South with a remark about the place of black people not in America but in the world; and that he insists, in the first essay, "Of Our Spiritual Strivings," that "Negro blood" has a message not just for America but (again) "for the world." Du Bois's cosmopolitanism overlays even the task of articulating a distinct black identity. He accepts the fundamental cosmopolitan moral idea that, whatever his duties to the Negro, he has obligations to those outside his racial horizon; and, finally, he is cosmopolitan in his methods, insisting on adopting a globally comparative perspective even when he is talking about the United States.

Du Bois sees the problem of Jim Crow, for example, as part of a global tragedy: the color line imposes

Jim Crow in Georgia, but it also imposes a destructive colonialism on what he regularly called, in one of his poetical formulations, "Asia and Africa . . . and the islands of the sea." The cosmopolitan imperative did not require, for Du Bois, a uniformity of outcome; it required simply that each race be permitted its full development. But what about the individuals subsumed in those groups? How would persons relate to peoples?

Humboldt's Gift

To grasp why W. E. B. Du Bois, drawing on the literary nationalism of the philosopher of the Sturm und Drang, could be an enthusiast both of personal individuality and of the development of "race groups," it helps to bring another romantic term into view: *Bildung,* or, to use John Stuart Mill's favorite translation, development. For Herder and his circle, development proceeded along two dimensions: the development of cultures as wholes and the development of persons within these cultures.

Wilhelm von Humboldt, whose engagement with Bildung had a practical as well as theoretical bent, advanced a kindred argument in somewhat greater detail. (The term also means "education," and, as we recall, Humboldt was Friedrich Wilhelm's education minister.) In the essay published as *The Limits of State Action*, written in the early 1790s, Humboldt addressed the question of how individual and collective development were related. Relationships, he argued, made it possible for us to draw open each other's cultural resources. But, he went on, "the utility of such relationships for Bildung entirely depends on the extent to which the independence of those in the relationships is maintained at the same time as the intimacy of the relationship."[25] While he conceded that—to speak in the language of individuality that we inherit from Romanticism—your being a German, or a Negro, could shape the authentic self whose expression is the project of your life, this was only consistent with real self-development if you could, at the same time, maintain your independence, your individuality.

There were educational implications, as well. The "true end of man," Humboldt avowed, was "the highest and most harmonious development of his powers to a whole."[26] For Humboldt, social harmony, too, was dependent upon "complete education," and he had thoughts about how the parts came together.

This complete education, he wrote, has a single essential foundation:

> The mind of the lowliest day-laborer must originally be attuned with the soul of the most finely cultivated person, if the former is not to fall beneath human dignity and become brutish, and the latter is not to become . . . sentimental, fantasyridden, and eccentric. . . . Even having learned Greek might, in this manner, be something as far from futile for the carpenter as making tables for the scholar.[27]

Almost a century later, scholars were still defending and disputing this vision. Schmoller, fencing with Treitschke, avowed, "The great progress of our age lies precisely in this: that it recognizes the honor of labor; that it no longer bluntly declares governing, painting and research to be the only things worthy of a decent man; that manual work and educational development are no longer regarded as excluding each other."[28]

These issues were anything but theoretical for Du Bois. Indeed, his famous debate with Booker T. Washington over the education of the Negro is essentially prefigured here. Washington's *Up from Slavery* conveyed palpable disdain for the sort of education Humboldt extolled. Describing the experience of teaching a class filled with students who were mostly public school teachers themselves, Washington wrote:

> The bigger the book and the longer the name of the subject, the prouder they felt of their accomplishment. Some had studied Latin, and one or two Greek. This they thought entitled them to special distinction.
>
> In fact, one of the saddest things I saw during the month of travel which I have described was a young man, who had attended some high school, sitting down in a one-room cabin, with grease on his clothing, filth all around him, and weeds in the yard and garden, engaged in studying a French grammar.[29]

In the year *The Souls of Black Folk* appeared, Washington boasted, in an essay on "Industrial Education for the Negro," that Tuskegee taught

> thirty-three trades and industries including carpentry, blacksmithing, printing, wheelwrighting, harnessmaking, painting, machinery, founding,

shoemaking, brickmasonry and brickmaking, plastering, sawmilling, tinsmithing, tailoring, mechanical and architectural drawing, electrical and steam engineering, canning, sewing, dressmaking, millinery, cooking, laundering, housekeeping, mattress making, basketry, nursing, agriculture, dairying and stock raising, and horticulture.

No mention of the Classics (the field in which Du Bois first taught) or philosophy or sociology or history or literature.[30] It was hard not to draw the inference that there was no need for more people with the Bildung of Dr. Du Bois. Du Bois's rejoinder was equally clear:

If we make money the object of man-training, we shall develop money-makers but not necessarily men; if we make technical skill the object of education, we may possess artisans but not, in nature, men. Men we shall have only as we make manhood the object of the work of the schools—intelligence, broad sympathy, knowledge of the world that was and is, and of the relation of men to it—this is the curriculum of that Higher Education which must underlie true life.

And he went on to add that "the object of all true education is not to make men carpenters, it is to make carpenters men."[31] Echoes of Humboldt's vision murmur through the text: Du Bois's carpenter, like Humboldt's, may have a use for Greek.

The "color-line" was to be condemned, accordingly, for depriving the people of the ability to cultivate fully their capacities—for hindering the Negroes' individual Bildung. From his earliest writings, Du Bois sought "the realization of that broader humanity which freely recognizes differences in men, but sternly deprecates inequality in their opportunities of development."[32] Again and again the language stresses, above all else, the value of education and self-development, for the individual and for the group.

Ethics and Community

The individual, Treitschke had said, "must forget his own I and feel himself a member of the whole"; and the sentiment would have resonated with Du Bois, whose 1897 Negro Academy address supposed that "200,000,000 black hearts beating in one glad song of jubilee" were needed for the Negro to gain true historical agency (that number meant to include all the people of African descent in the world). Such rhetoric of communion might seem to leave no room for moral autonomy, let alone individuality—even if Du Bois did not go on to say, with Treitschke, that the same individual "should recognize how much his life is nothing over against the Wellbeing of the whole."[33] But no student of the Harvard Hegelians would have drawn that conclusion.

In "A Study in Self-Sacrifice," which appeared a year before *The Souls of Black Folk,* George Herbert Palmer offered a cautionary example. He recalls a story from the Civil War, in which an officer finds a "cowardly fellow," just before battle, sneaking back to camp. "Turning upon him in a passion of disgust, he said, 'What! Do you count your miserable little life worth more than that of this great army?' 'Worth more to me, sir,' the man replied." Palmer's gloss on this episode is worth citing at length:

How sensible! How entirely just from his own point of view, that of the isolated self! Taking only this into account, he was but a moral child, incapable of comprehending anything so difficult as a conjunct self. He imagined that could he but save this eating, breathing, feeling self, no matter if the country were lost, he would be a gainer. What folly! What would existence be worth outside the total interrelationship of human beings called his land? But this fact he could not perceive.[34]

The "conjunct self," for Palmer, was the only self worth having.

The search for a proper balance between the local and the universal can be found as well in the contemporaneous writings of Josiah Royce. In "The Spirit of Modern Philosophy" (1892), he expresses his view on the question in a rather ontological-sounding proposition: "I become myself by forsaking my isolation and by entering into community."[35] But a more explicitly political turn can be found in Royce's later work. In the same year Palmer published his essay on "Self-Sacrifice," Royce defended what he called, with deliberate provocation, "provincialism" in an address to the Phi Beta Kappa Society at the University of Iowa. By provincialism, he said, he meant, first, the tendency of "a province to possess its own customs and ideals; secondly, the totality of these customs and ideals themselves; and thirdly, the love and pride which leads the inhabitants of a province to cherish as their own these traditions, beliefs, and aspirations."

Royce considered it "a saving power to which the world in the near future will need more and more to appeal."[36] It's hugely important that the will of the individual doesn't disappear in this account. Indeed, the individual who freely allies himself with larger social groups is central to Royce's vision. The sort of provincialism he was commending, Royce explains in *The Philosophy of Loyalty* (1908), was "the sort of provincialism that makes people want to idealize, to adorn, to ennoble, to educate, their own province."[37] Loyalty was thus the "willing and thoroughgoing devotion of a self to a cause."[38] He knew that we no more choose our causes than we choose our values; in some measure, they choose us. And yet we could consciously identify with them or reject them. Thus

> all of the higher types of loyalty involve autonomous choice. The cause that is to appeal to me at all must indeed have some elemental fascination for me. It must stir me, arouse me, please me, and in the end possess me. Moreover, it must, indeed, be set before me by my social order as a possible, a

practically significant, a living cause, which binds many selves in the unity of one life.[39]

Royce's defense of provincialism, accordingly, came with a recognition of the dangers of what he called "false forms of provincialism."[40] Sectionalism was one kind of danger; the Civil War was fought, he says, to overcome this evil. And he worried about antisocial forms of sociability, about "our American intolerance" toward foreigners. Du Bois, for his part, always recognized the risk that black folk, facing a world in which so many of the white people they met would disdain them, would withdraw from contact across nations and peoples, the contact that the cosmopolitan claims is vivifying and essential. He makes the point in *Dusk of Dawn,* when he talks of the way American racism imprisons black people within the race:

Practically, this group imprisonment within a group has various effects upon the prisoner. He becomes provincial and centered upon the problems of his particular group. He tends to neglect the wider aspects of national life and human existence. On the one hand he is unselfish so far as his inner group is concerned. He thinks of himself not as an individual but as a group man, a "race" man. His loyalty to this group idea tends to be almost unending and balks at almost no sacrifice. On the other hand, his attitude toward the environing race congeals into a matter of unreasoning resentment and even hatred, deep disbelief in them and refusal to conceive honesty and rational thought on their part. This attitude adds to the difficulties of conversation, intercourse, understanding between groups.[41]

Notice that what Du Bois says here about black people enclosed within America could be applied equally to Americans who, in their blinkered nationalism, close themselves off to the world. This formulation seems deliberately abstract: it is a general critique of the anticosmopolitan tendencies of one strand of nationalism. And indeed, in the 1920 essay "The Souls of White Folk," Du Bois expressed pity, in very much the same terms, for white Americans "imprisoned and enthralled, hampered and made miserable" by racism.[42]

Yet Du Bois's cosmopolitanism was not the bloodless rejection of locality that inspired some of his contemporaries.[43] In *Souls,* in the essay "Of the Meaning of Progress," he writes with real tenderness of his time as a teacher in the rural South, evoking "the soft melody and mighty cadences of Negro song" in church on Sundays, the "half-awakened common consciousness, sprung from common joy and grief, at burial, birth, or wedding; from a common hardship in poverty, poor land, and low wages." Nothing could be more sympathetic than his evocation of life in a Liberian village at his first visit to the African continent in *Dusk of Dawn.*

> Then we came to the village; how can I describe it? Neither London, nor Paris, nor New York has anything of its delicate, precious beauty. It was a town of the Veys and done in cream and pale purple—still, clean, restrained, tiny, complete. It was no selfish place, but the central abode of fire and hospitality, clean-swept for wayfarers, and best seats were bare.

Du Bois was as fully aware of the attractions of rootedness as he was of its limitations.[44]

So far, we've been discussing the ways Du Bois aligned moral universalism with a special devotion to a group, ways that belong to a matrix of ideas in the worlds in which he was educated. We have seen that he had a conception of the self as inseparable from community; a conception of meaningful striving as taking place within such communities; and a conception of those groups as gift-bearing members of a larger world of such groups, whether nations or cultures or races. It would be a mistake, however, to suppose that Du Bois had simply arrived at a harmonious equilibrium between the ideals of racial and of individual Bildung. At times, these too could seem like "two warring ideals in one dark body."

He had been trained by Schmoller to resist methodological individualism, to grant the reality and agency of race or nation as a social fact, and in "The Conservation of Races" he pushes the collectivist rhetoric to its limits. Our task, he writes there, is "the development of these race groups not as individuals but as races." We must not be misled by the "individualistic philosophy of the Declaration of Independence and the laissez-faire philosophy of Adam Smith." At moments, he pushes past Schmoller to embrace Treitschkean organicism in full flow: The great men of history are merely "epitomized impressions" of vast races. "The history of the world is the history, not of individuals, but of groups, not of nations, but of races, and he who ignores or seeks to override the race idea in human history ignores and overrides the central thought of all history."[45]

And yet, and yet. Du Bois was also given to writing of himself as a heroic isolate, alone in his sorrow and the crafter of his fate. Recounting his Age of Miracles, in *Darkwater,* he captures this mood perfectly: "I was captain of my soul and master of my fate! I *willed* to do! It was done. I *wished!* The wish came true." In his essay "The Superior Race" (1923), he warns against the temptation to suppose that groups have "integrating souls," as human beings do. "They have not," he says. "The soul is still individual if it is free."[46] It's a startling claim from the author of *The Souls of Black Folk,* and suggests that this title can be read in two ways—as *the souls of a black people* and as *the souls of black people.* Perhaps we are to think both of the souls of individual black folk and of multiple souls contending for possession of the collective black folk. The truth is that Du Bois pulses with individualist and collectivist rhetoric, in an alternating current. This Methodenstreit runs through him.

Verstehen

Du Bois found a rich seam, too, in another methodological crevasse. Wilhelm Dilthey, with whom Du
Bois took a seminar on the history of philosophy in
the summer semester of 1893, was at pains to distinguish between the methods proper to the natural sciences, *Naturwissenschaften,* on the one hand, and those
proper to the human sciences, the *Geisteswissenschaften,*
on the other. In particular, he warned against the
temptation (which afflicted much Enlightenment
thought, but also later forms of scientism) to model
the second on the first. And he went on to make a
powerful suggestion. Psychological experience, he
proposed, was a matter not of explanation, *erklären,*
but of understanding—*verstehen*. "Nature we explain,
but psychic life we understand," was Dilthey's formulation. A chemical reaction was to be explained; a
historical figure was to be understood. We had to try
to get inside the person's head, to take on his or her
perspective: in a sense, to relive the experiences of
others, via a *Nachbild,* a sort of afterimage, of those
experiences.[47] Your grief, for example, is externalized
in your grief-stricken expression; I understand your

grief when my experience of your expression is internalized through my Nachbild of your experience.[48] Verstehen—as opposed to both explanation and to observation, Schmoller's geschehen—implied an interpretive, first-personal perspective, one that aspired, via intuition and empathy, to the immediacy with which you relate to your own mental life—your own experiences, sense of self, and sense of community. Dilthey's proposal has been much parsed, but—along with his holism, emphasis on the nonrational, and resistance to positivism and reductionism—it was extremely influential in the years preceding the First World War.

Du Bois's disciplinary schizophrenia, his own alternation between soaring, rhapsodic poeticism and dry, assiduous empiricism, might seem a response to Dilthey's distinction. Throughout his career, he struggled with the parallax that arose from sharing the insider's perspective and the outsider's perspective, the subject's view and the scholar's. The Negro problem, for Du Bois, was to be the subject of observation and explanation, in the Schmollerian mode. And yet "facts, in social science, I realized, were elusive things."[49] How could he convey what it was like to be a Negro in America with the usual apparatus of social-scientific research? Could the mere recitation of fact ever capture the reality of a bloody race riot, or of a Negro revival in the Southern backwoods? Verstehen, the subjective evocation of lived experience, would have to complement Schmoller's geschehen.

Hence those whiplashing shifts of register within *The Souls of Black Folk*. On one page we get a dry recitation of the particulars; we may learn that, according to a recent study of Negro college graduates, "fifty-three per cent . . . were teachers,—presidents of institutions, heads of normal schools, principals of city school systems, and the like. Seventeen per cent were clergymen; another seventeen per cent were in the professions, chiefly as physicians. Over six per cent were merchants, farmers, and artisans, and four per cent were in the government civil service." On another page, evoking a revival meeting, Du Bois gives us this:

A sort of suppressed terror hung in the air and seemed to seize us,—a pythian madness, a demoniac possession, that lent terrible reality to song and word. The black and massive form of the preacher swayed and quivered as the words crowded to his

lips and flew at us in singular eloquence. The
people moaned and fluttered, and then the gaunt-
cheeked brown woman beside me suddenly leaped
straight into the air and shrieked like a lost soul,
while round about came wail and groan and
outcry.[50]

This wild alternation of voice did not go unremarked. Du Bois's sometime friend and collaborator
Kelly Miller astutely described him as "a man of re-
markable amplitude and contrariety of qualities, an
exact interrogator and a lucid expositor of social reality, but withal a dreamer with a fantasy of mind that
verges on 'the fine frenzy.'" He marveled that someone capable of such careful scholarship should also be
in possession of a mind "cast in a weird and fantastic
mold."[51] This is not, to be sure, what Dilthey had in
mind. His methodological proposals were an attempt
to make a science of verstehen: he wanted to discipline our subjectivity, not to set it free.[52] Du Bois, at
his soberest, wanted both the discipline of fact explained and the discipline of experience understood;
occasionally, though, he wrote as if he thought that
verstehen required an escape from reason. He evidently considered both modes necessary for his larger

project. Investigating the American counterpart to the Soziale Frage, namely, "the question of questions, the Negro problem,"[53] he often aspired, as we saw, to Schmollerian empiricism, the primacy of the geschehen. But this approach, he knew, captured only half the picture. As Dilthey had argued, in order to grasp why, say, Caesar crossed the Rubicon, we had to be prepared to ask the question: How did it feel to be Caesar? Du Bois, transposing two domains, was thus led to pose a question that had never quite been posed before: "How does it feel to be a problem?"

CHAPTER THREE

The Concept of the Negro

> Take, for instance, the answer to the apparently
> simple question "What is a Negro?" We find
> the most extraordinary confusion of
> thought and difference of opinion.
> —W. E. B. Du Bois, *The Negro*

We have been exploring the intellectual underpin-
nings of Du Bois's project of racial advancement, the
conceptual matrix in which it grew. We've examined
his strategies of scholarly engagement; his aesthetic,
moral, and methodological cosmopolitanism; his ideas
of culture and spirit and striving. But so far we have
merely circled his central preoccupation: the idea of
race itself.

Du Bois's first programmatic discussion of the subject was in "The Conservation of Races," a paper he
gave at the second meeting of the American Negro
Academy, which was published as the second of the
academy's Occasional Papers in 1897. There he urged

his audience that they should "seriously consider" this question: "What is the real meaning of Race?" He answered, first, that, "The final word of science, so far, is that we have at least two, perhaps three, great families of human beings—the whites and Negroes, possibly the yellow race."[1] He is speaking during the full flowering of scientific racism. The French count Arthur de Gobineau posited just those three races in his *Essay on the Inequality of Races*) (1853–1855), arguing for polygenesis, the view that they did not even share a common ancestor; the distinguished Darwinian Ernst Haeckel, a Prussian anatomist, argued in 1878 that there were twelve; the German-born naturalist Carl Vogt—who mentions Egyptians, Jews, Tatars, Scythians, the races of Assyria and India, Negroes, Berbers, Greeks, Persians, Arabs, and Turks in a single paragraph of his *Lectures on Man*—would have given us more.[2]

Treitschke, for his part, remarked in his *Politics* that although there were many races, "for the historian only the white, black, red, and yellow races come into consideration."[3] But a page or two later he is insisting on a distinction, within the white race, between Aryans and Semites, and suggesting, on the other hand, that red and yellow are a single stock.[4] And while he calls the Germans a nation, not a race, it is not at all clear what the principle of demarcation is: when he is discussing the interactions of Germans and Magyars, on the one hand, and Slovaks and Vlachs, on the other, in Austria, he calls it a meeting of *two* races.[5] (What *is* clear is that Treitschke believes the Germans, nation or race, are warriors with a historical destiny to subjugate their inferiors, especially the Slavs.) So Du Bois's talk of these "great families of human beings" was nothing if not conventional in form, whatever was new in its substance.

What matters for Du Bois about these races that science has discerned, however, is not the "grosser physical differences of color, hair and bone" but the "differences—subtle, delicate and elusive, though they may be—which have silently but definitely separated men into groups."

While these subtle forces have generally followed the natural cleavage of common blood, descent and physical peculiarities, they have at other times swept across and ignored these. At all times, however, they have divided human beings into races, which, while they perhaps transcend scientific definition, nevertheless, are clearly defined to the eye of the historian and sociologist.

Even in 1897, then, Du Bois is resisting the biological model: the subtle forces are not reducible to shared bloodlines, but sometimes run athwart them; races "perhaps transcend scientific definition."

What then is a race? It is a vast family of human beings, generally of common blood and language, always of common history, traditions and impulses, who are both voluntarily and involuntarily striving together for the accomplishment of certain more or less vividly conceived ideals of life.

And, on Du Bois's view, once we look with the eye of the historian and sociologist, there are not three but eight "distinctly differentiated races, in the sense in which history tells us the word must be used." They are "the Slavs of eastern Europe, the Teutons of middle Europe, the English of Great Britain and America, the Romance nations of Southern and Western Europe, the Negroes of African and America, the Semitic people of Western Asia and Northern Africa, the Hindoos of Central Asia, and the Mongolians of Eastern Asia."[6]

It is a measure of the instability of the term "race" in Du Bois's language that this list of eight is different from the list of the six racial brothers plus the Negro "seventh son" in "Strivings of the Negro People," published the very same year. To see why this is, we must read further: "The question now is: What is the real distinction between these nations? Is it physical differences of blood, color and cranial measurements?"

Du Bois admits, first, that physical differences "play a great part," but goes on to argue that the real differences between races cannot be understood in these physical terms; nor can mere physical properties explain the elective affinities of members of each race for their fellows. No, he insists, "the deeper differences are spiritual, psychical, differences—undoubtedly based on the physical, but infinitely transcending them."[7]

Notice how easily Du Bois slips between talk of "race" and talk of "nation" in these passages, in ways we have seen in Treitschke already. The logical point here is quite simple: once you use the word "race" for groups of common descent, you can, so to speak, narrow or broaden your focus on the human family tree. When Haeckel treats Semites and Indo-Europeans as both members of his Mediterranean race, he is looking broadly; but Semites and Indo-Europeans can also be races as the focus narrows.

From our contemporary point of view, Du Bois's historical "races" are an odd assortment. Slavic, English, Romance, Negro, Semitic, Hindu, Mongolian: these, apparently, are the families of man revealed to the social scientific vision. The three races—black, white, and yellow—are replaced, once we take this historical view, by eight groups of which only one, the English, is uncontroversially a nation in the modern sense (even though Du Bois takes it to be spread over two continents). Two of the groups, German and Slav, though not juridical nations, had Pan-German and Pan-Slavist nationalist movements in place that might have wanted them to be so; two—Romance and Semite—are more readily seen as zones of shared culture; and three—Negro, Hindu, and Mongolian— are neither nations nor cultures but vast assemblages of both. You could almost suppose that this schema was a deliberate piece of mischief.

At other moments, though, his conception is deeply romantic, and there is absolutely no doubt about the seriousness with which he treats the ethical meaning of race. Nowhere is this more true than in the passage that ends this discussion, in the lines I quoted earlier: all these nations, he says, are—note the word again— "striving, each in its own way, to develop for civilization its particular message, its particular ideal, which shall help guide the world nearer and nearer that perfection of human life for which we all long, that 'one far-off Divine event.'"[8] (You can be sure that a late Victorian writer is in earnest when he quotes Tennyson.)

Du Bois's account here of racial or national membership is focused on the ideas—or, as we might also say, the principles—expressed in the collective life of a people; and in insisting on this, he is thinking about national history in the way that would have been familiar to him. It was, after all, the standard understanding of Hegel's philosophy of history: that human experience was the working out of an idea—in fact of something called *the* Idea—in history.[9] In the less metaphysical version of the story, which Du Bois borrows not from the philosophers but from the historians, nations are the historical expressions not of one grand universal Idea but of slightly less grand particular ideas. The English nation stands, Du Bois says in a perfectly conventional formulation, for "constitutional liberty and commercial freedom"; the German nation for "science and philosophy"; the Romance nations for "literature and art." If these are the capital-I Ideas of those peoples, Du Bois is searching for the Negro Idea.

> The full, complete Negro message of the whole Negro race has not as yet been given to the world . . .
>
> The question is, then: how shall this message be delivered; how shall these various ideals be realized? The answer is plain: by the development of these race groups, not as individuals, but as races . . . only . . . Negroes inspired by one vast ideal, can work out in its fullness the great message we have for humanity.[10]

For us, now, the word "race" still suggests a form of membership that can be defined independently of politics, while "nation" suggests a form of belonging that is, at the very least, ambitious for political recognition and, at the most, depends on a connection to a state. Even in Du Bois's day, "race" was the more natural term to use for a group that crossed states or societies, "nation" the more obvious word when questions of ethnoterritorial loyalty were in play. We can see the importance of the independence of race from any actual political affiliations if we ask a question that he and his contemporaries might have thought strange: Why did Du Bois think he had anything in common with people raised in an entirely different culture and climate on a continent thousands of miles away, a continent on which, in 1897, he had, as yet, not set foot? A biological account would have provided a ready explanation for the unity of the Negro people. But we already saw—from that easy movement between talk of race and talk of nation, from his insistence that "physical" similarities were not crucial—that Du Bois sought a different account. What was crucial, he thought, were those "ideals of life."

The romantic notion of a collective and involuntary striving for an ideal doesn't make much sense to us now, if it ever did. We think this is one of the more misleading consequences of the idea that nations have souls. But there is something important in the implication that races matter because membership in a race allows people—compels people—to work together for common purposes. Here we find glimmers of what Royce would call "loyalty to loyalty," which characterized a cause that was "good, not only for me, but for mankind."[11]

It is thus quite proper to speak of Du Bois's attitude to his racial identity as a form of nationalism: he believed about the Negro race everything that an American patriot of his day would have believed about America (or a German about Germany), except that he did not believe that it required a single country, a nation-state, to gather its people in. So he believed in a Negro national character and a Negro national destiny; and he thought it was the duty of black people—especially of the most talented black people—to work together in the service of the Negro people. As he had put it in the Academy Creed, with which he ended the "Conservation of Races,"

1. We believe that the Negro people, as a race, have a contribution to make to civilization and humanity, which no other race can make.

2. We believe it the duty of the Americans of Negro descent, as a body, to maintain their race identity until this mission of the Negro people is accomplished, and the ideal of human brotherhood has become a practical possibility.[12]

The Negro national character bestowed upon black folk special gifts—the gifts of the "seventh son"—but it was their duty to develop these gifts and deliver their special contribution to all mankind. Once this had happened, however, their "race identity" need no longer be husbanded; it could disappear without harm. In the very course of insisting upon the ethical salience of race, then, he also remarks on its perishability.

In distancing himself from scientific racism he was, as I said, moving against the grain of much nineteenth-century thought. But he was moving *with* the grain of other intellectual strains with which he was familiar. In the preface to his *Weltgeschichte,* which first appeared in 1883, Leopold von Ranke—the most influential German historian of the era—cautions, ever the empiricist of the *eigentlich gewesen* (what actually happened), against the theoretical rush to racial determinism: "Nationalities of such great power and such distinctive character as the English or the Italian are not so much creations of the soil and the race as of great changes in events."[13] So not all humanists were beguiled by the new ethnology. There were more powerful arguments for skepticism on offer, however.

Words and Things

Consider Hermann Lotze, a founder of neo-Kantian thought and an authority cited regularly by Du Bois's professors, notably William James and Schmoller.[14] Royce studied with Lotze; Santayana's doctoral dissertation was a critique of Lotze. Someone with Du Bois's education could hardly have avoided him. Lotze, who was trained in medicine as well as in philosophy, was both fascinated by the natural sciences and mindful of their limits; guided by Kant's distinction between the *Sinnenwelt* and the *Verstandeswelt* (unhelpfully but inevitably translated as the "sensible world" and the "intelligible world"), he sought to mark out questions that were and were not subject to empirical determination. In *Microcosmus: Ideas on the Natural History and the History of Humanity, Attempt at an Anthropology* (1856–1864), he delves into the natural history of race and the ongoing debates between monogenesis and polygenesis. Did the different branches of humanity have a common origin or not?

His discussion is striking for a number of reasons. For one thing, he suggests that the giant and creaky apparatus of race, at least as conceived in polygenetic terms, rested upon the most superficial of all distinctions, the variations of skin hue. "Certainly, if Nature had not colored the Negro black, the Indian red," ordinary people would not have found in their other features "a reason to treat them as different kinds of men and to deny them common origins," he observed.[15] Indeed, Lotze calls into question the moral and metaphysical significance of descent. He asks us to consider what would follow from the discovery of verifiable evidence that "the ancestors of the Negro really were true indubitable apes," given that we know from experience that present-day Negroes are "possessed of intelligence, be it great or small, and of the capacity to walk upright, to speak and to think."

> What moral excuse would there be for the cruelty of not treating them according to what they are, but according to what their ancestors were—or, to put the matter logically, according to the kind or species to which they belong by their ancestry? Or, if it now were certain, conversely, that the apes were stunted human beings, whose ancestors we perhaps meet in human form in the history of past times, would it not still remain the case, that they now are nevertheless only really apes?[16]

The discussion takes place in a chapter entitled "Varieties of the Human Race." But his larger purpose eventually becomes clear. Lotze wants us to rethink *all* our assumptions about kinds. He takes aim, in particular, at the way we distinguish between "the concept of a natural kind or species and a variant or variety," which underlies the arguments over whether the races are "only variants of one species, not different species of one genus." These disputes amount to no more than "a logical game of formulas," he says. It doesn't matter what name we use for these distinctions. "Variety" as applied to the forms of humanity "is a title without emoluments," and the whole debate over species and varieties is a matter of "logical prolixities" that "decide nothing."[17] (We are not so far from Du Bois's characterization, in *Dusk of Dawn,* of later attempts to model society on biology: "fruitless word-twisting."[18]) What's more, Lotze's inclination was to diminish the significance of human variation: "If Nature is to maintain barriers between the individual kinds of her creatures, there must somewhere be a difference in shaping impulses that excludes the creation of intermediate forms"—which is obviously contrary to fact.[19] (Lotze's views on the mulatto, by the way, make an interesting contrast with Treitschke's: he supposed that interracial mixing could produce people of real intellectual gifts.)[20]

Lotzean thought adumbrates a far-reaching skepticism about classification. He warned about reification, about the way the adjective "beautiful," say, can license misleading, mystified talk of "the Beautiful," and he pointed to other cases where—through mistaking "the newly acquired syntactic dignity of words" for a "metaphysical dignity" of the associated concepts—"language creates for us a mythology."[21] More sweepingly, in a discussion of nominalism and realism in his *Logic,* he maintains that classifications have "no real significance in relation to the actual structure and development of things themselves." We can, on the contrary, choose to "subsume the same object S under different general notions, or to construct its conception of the object by means of several widely divergent series of successful determinations. In such a case we are at liberty to ask with a view to the particular purpose of any enquiry, which of these various constructions is to be preferred."[22] Here, Lotze anticipates a rich vein of pragmatist skepticism about natural kinds—in particular, the pragmatist insistence that we attend to the purpose or interests served by a system of classification.[23] You can see why William James, a self-described "radical empiricist" who inveighed against what he called the scientific "veto" in the cultural realm, had an affinity for Lotze. And why Schmoller, with his inveterate distrust of the "natural" in historical explanation, should have found in him an ally.

Du Bois's immersion in historicism, too, would have encouraged skepticism toward the new racial ethnology. Dilthey—who, when Lotze died, was given his chair at Berlin—was professionally inclined to distrust notions that historians had imported from the natural sciences. And so it was with race: "When historical deeds and destinies are interwoven into [a] genealogical articulation, *peoples* or *nations* are formed," he writes, in a passage that combines concession and resistance. "They are the living and relatively independent centers of culture within the social context of a time and are the carriers of historical movement. A people has its natural genealogical roots which can be recognized physically. But while related peoples show a kinship of somatic types which maintains itself with marvelous constancy, their historical and spiritual physiognomy creates ever more refined differences in all the various spheres of the life of a people."[24] Recall Du Bois's talk of "subtle forces," his insistence that "no mere physical distinction would really define or explain the deeper differences—the cohesiveness and continuity of these groups."[25]

Dilthey praised Herder as the founder of historicism but did not exempt the great historicist from historicist scrutiny. He saw mysticism in Herder's free use of such ahistorical notions as spirit and soul. Dilthey wrote,

> The individual unit of life in a people that is manifested in the affinity of all its life expression, such as its law, language, and religion, is mystically expressed in terms such as *Volksseele* (soul of a people), *Nation, Volksgeist* (spirit of a people), "country," and "organism." But these concepts are no more usable in history than is the concept of lifeforce in physiology.[26]

Still, Dilthey wasn't rejecting the notion of a "unity of life in a people"; the aim was to make such notions more rigorous by engaging in the work of theoretical and historical interrogation. He was saving Herder by reforming him. Nor did he suppose that exposing the social forces that produced our ideas would make those ideas disappear. In the end, we had to engage with the social world in the terms it mobilized.

That was what Du Bois was doing at the American
Negro Academy. In order to conserve race, this "ingenious invention for human progress," he wanted to
replace the biological conception with a historical
and sociological one—and to do so without robbing
the term of its social efficacy. He would try to resist
talk of fixed traits, even the fixed inheritance of Herderian Kultur. Instead, his providential rhetoric conveyed the idea that the meaning of his race would
unfold through a process of social interaction, participation, striving—in short, through history.[27]

Science against Racism

For all that, Du Bois was attentive to the scientific
research into human diversity. If scientific racism
was, as he thought, bad science, it would need to be
exposed as such. Here the anthropologist Franz Boas
(who left the Royal Ethnographic Museum in Berlin
to move to New York five years before Du Bois arrived at the Friedrich-Wilhelm University) played a
significant role. Boas's careful empirical fieldwork undermined many of the claims about race and about
cultural development that dominated the writings of
earlier geographers and natural historians, and Du

Bois was clearly aware of these scholarly developments. In 1906, Du Bois invited Boas, who was then a professor of anthropology at Columbia, to give a commencement address at Atlanta University. Boas, guided empirically by historical and ethnographic evidence, and theoretically by the new recognition of the variability within populations, spoke with great force and confidence:

> To those who stoutly maintain a material inferiority of the Negro race . . . , you may confidently reply that the burden of proof rests with them, that the past history of your race does not sustain their statement, but rather gives you encouragement. The physical inferiority of the Negro race, if it exists at all, is insignificant when compared to the wide range of individual variability in each race. There is no anatomical evidence available that would sustain the view that the bulk of the Negro race could not become as useful citizens as the members of any other race. That there may be slightly different hereditary traits seems plausible, but it is entirely arbitrary to assume that those of the Negro, because perhaps slightly different, must be of an inferior type.[28]

In the very same year, Du Bois wrote:

We have, then, in the so-called Negro races to do
with a great variety of human types and mixtures
of blood representing at bottom a human variation
which separated from the primitive human stock
some ages after the yellow race and before the Mediterranean race, and which has since intermingled
with these races in all degrees of admixture so that
today no absolute separating line can be drawn.[29]

(Notice that Du Bois follows Haeckel here in referring to the white race as "Mediterranean.")

In the same essay, Du Bois quotes a passage from
Friedrich Ratzel's *The History of Mankind,* which appeared in English in 1897, to reinforce his claim that
one could no longer speak scientifically of a pure Negro type:

The name "Negro" originally embraces one of the
most unmistakable conceptions of ethnology—the
African with dark skin, so-called "woolly" hair,
thick lips and nose; and it is one of the prodigious,
nay amazing achievements of critical erudition to
have latterly confined this (and that even in Africa,
the genuine old Negro country) to a small district.

Ratzel goes on to cite a variety of scholarly sources for distinguishing genuine Negroes from "Gallas, Nubians, Hottentots, Kaffirs, the Congo races, and the Malagasies," on the one hand, and "Shillooks and Bongos" and "light-colored South Africans, and the Bantu or Kaffir peoples," on the other.

> Nothing then remains for the Negroes in the pure sense of the word save, as Waitz says, "a tract of country extending over not more than 10 or 12 degrees of latitude, which may be traced from the mouth of the Senegal river to Timbuctoo, and thence extended to the regions about Sennaar." Even in this the race reduced to these dimensions is permeated by a number of people belonging to other stocks. According to Latham, indeed, the real Negro country extends only from the Senegal to the Niger.[30]

Du Bois is quoting the authoritative summary of an eminent German scholar to underline the point that the dark-skinned people of Africa are extremely diverse even in their phenotypic characteristics. (By the 1960s, as global genetic diversity began to be measured, it was clear that Africa was, in essence, the most biologically diverse of the continents, so far as our species is concerned, as would be expected of the place to which all modern humanity traces its roots. After all, humanity outside Africa is descended from a relatively recent sampling of the genomes of the core of the original African population of *Homo sapiens.*[31])

In *The Crisis,* Du Bois regularly shared his changing understanding with a wider world of black intellectuals. In 1911, for example, he published an essay drawing lessons from the proceedings of the First Universal Races Congress in London. Within weeks of the Congress, Du Bois told his readers that, according to "the leading scientists of the world," it is "not legitimate to argue from differences in physical characteristics to differences in mental characteristics," and that "the civilization of a . . . race at any particular moment of time offers no index to its innate or inherited capacities."[32]

What we see here is early evidence of a tectonic shift in the scientific thinking about race. Mendel's ideas were rediscovered around 1900. By 1915, the zoologist Thomas H. Morgan had published, with his coauthors, *The Mechanism of Mendelian Heredity,* based in large measure on work on the inheritance of mutations in the fruit fly he made famous, *Drosophila mela-*

nogaster. The astonishing advances in genetics—a term coined by William Bateson at Cambridge around 1905—in the first two decades of the century forced a general rethinking of the biology of heritable characteristics. Within a generation there was a synthesis of Mendelian genetics and Darwinian evolutionary theory in the work of population geneticists led by J. B. S. Haldane, R. A. Fisher, and Sewall Wright. (It is perhaps the most important work in twentieth-century biology that was not recognized with a Nobel.) This union of Mendelian and Darwinian ideas—one whose broad features remain part of the contemporary scientific picture—received its canonical expression in Sir Julian Huxley's elegant 1942 book *Evolution: The Modern Synthesis.*

At the same time, people were starting to think differently about the relationship between biology and culture. The new population genetics made it easier to see that, even when psychological properties had a genetic component, they could be inherited independent of the physical characteristics that visibly distinguished those with darker skin from those with lighter-skin, or those with kinky hair from those whose hair was straight. This established theoretically something you could have noticed by empirical observation—that there was no necessary connection between bodily phenotype and mental capacity—and so undermined one of the central premises of late nineteenth-century racial condescension. Characteristics could be attributed to individual genes, transmitted independently, if they were on different chromosomes, but separable in principle (by the exchange of parts among chromosomes in "crossing over") even if they were not. As a result, it was now conceptually clear that there was not likely to be a single underlying genetic property (however many genes it involved) that Negroes—or Caucasians or Mongols or Teutons or Celts—shared.

There is, in other words, biological variation within the races, however we define them; and it can include variation, by mutation or by inheritance, in any characteristics, save (as a matter of stipulation) those that we use to define the race in the first place. If we end up by defining a race as consisting of people of common ancestry—which means they are descended from people who once interbred in some *place* in the past—then there is, in fact, no reason even to insist that there is any hereditary factor they must all bear that is not borne by some or all people whose ancestors lived elsewhere.

So the idea of internal variation within races is built into the Mendelian elements of this new picture; and Du Bois (like Boas) shows that he recognizes this by insisting regularly on this variation. Darwin had himself reached the conclusion that human races displayed internal variability by extensive exposure to the widest range of human beings, as he voyaged on *The Beagle.* "Savages," he wrote in *The Descent of Man,* "even within the limits of the same tribe, are not nearly so uniform in character, as has often been said."[33] But equipped with the genetic theory that Darwin lacked, Du Bois insists with Ratzel on denying that there is a single Negro type, not, like Darwin, out of mere empiricism: he does it, I think, because he grasped a new insight made possible by a new biological theory.

Some drew the conclusion—and many still do— that at this point there is no longer any reason to take racial groupings seriously. If the properties that members of a race all share are only the superficial phenotypic ones that we use, in social life, to assign people to these categories, they have, precisely, only superficial things in common. Du Bois, of course, did not draw that conclusion. As we have just seen, he understood far earlier than most European and American intellectuals that the Western race-concept could not be elucidated in purely biological terms—that membership in a common race did not guarantee that you were bound together through the common expression of shared underlying, inheritable properties. Nevertheless, he believed that there was something that members of a race shared; and he thought that something was interesting and important enough to make being-a-Negro central to his own self-conception. What could that something else be?

Subtle Forces

Once we have the Mendelian picture, we can distinguish between two ways people of common descent can inherit properties from their ancestors. One way is through bodily inheritance, through the transmission of genes. This is the literal meaning of the metaphor of "common blood." Each new generation is a sampling and mixture of the genes of the previous generation. But another way each generation is shaped by earlier ones is through cultural transmission. And because the central mechanism here operates through language and other forms of public behavior, it can cross the boundaries of populations defined by common descent. Du Bois's English race, for example, if it were defined through English as a language—a cultural form—would now include large numbers of people in India, Africa, and Southeast Asia, whose ancestors have never lived in the British Isles. In the new picture, we can ask whether the "subtle forces" that distinguish races are biological or cultural (or both). And Du Bois's division of the field of study between natural science and the human sciences— history and sociology—shows that, even before he had the new picture, he was arguing that races were primarily shaped by culture.

So what is it that the historian and sociologist see so clearly? In these disciplines as Du Bois conceived of them, what is visible is, first of all, not so much the property of individuals but of groups. The *individual* variation within groups that, as I argued earlier, he lays great stress on, doesn't mean that the *groups* do not display distinguishable general properties. Indeed, even if there are members of the Negro race who are biologically much more like some Caucasians than they are like most Negroes, Negroes as a group could still differ from Caucasians as a group. One property of Negroes as a group, to pick an uninteresting example, is their average height. And that can be different from the average height of Caucasians even if many Negroes are the same height as many Caucasians. More interestingly, a racial group is a social group; and distinct social groups can obviously sustain distinct cultural practices, even though they have members who have a great deal in common physically with members of other groups.

Once more, there is a simple conceptual point here that the new biological understanding, with its division of cultural from biological transmission, made it possible to see with great clarity. Even if a group is defined by a shared heritable physical characteristic, that characteristic doesn't have to be what accounts for everything the group has in common. As long as people recognize each other as fellow members by way of their visible characteristics, and especially if others do so as well, they can act together through that recognition. Indeed, there can be members of the group who do not share the defining physical characteristic: people, like light-complected black people, whose membership derives from the fact that their recent ancestors or others in their family do have it. As long as this fact is enough to bind them into the group, they do not even need to share the feature— blackness—that actually defines the group in the cultural imagination. And once the group exists in the cultural imagination, it can develop, through cultural transmission, a shared character, in part by shaping the behavior of its individual members. When Du Bois said the forces were "subtle," I think he was glimpsing, if not, perhaps, articulating clearly, that they were *not* physical. The new picture made it possible to see clearly how this could be: how a group defined by common blood could share characteristics that were nevertheless not inherited in the blood. And, with Dilthey in mind, he could see the group's nature as the subject of verstehen as much as of erklären.

So in 1920, he could assert, "There are no races, in the sense of great, separate, pure breeds of men, differing in attainment, development, and capacity."[34] In 1923, he held that the group has only the properties of its members—that a "a certain group that I know and to which I belong . . . bears in its bosom just now the spiritual hope of this land because of the persons who compose it and not by divine command." (As we've noticed, Du Bois's argument for racial solidarity, however tempered by cosmopolitan openness, often took on a providential air.) And by the time we get to *Dusk of Dawn*—the "essay toward the autobiography of a race concept" he published at the beginning of the Second World War—Du Bois asserts bluntly:

> It is easy to see that scientific definition of race is impossible; it is easy to prove that physical characteristics are not so inherited as to make it possible to divide the world into races; that ability is the monopoly of no known aristocracy; that the possibilities of human development cannot be circumscribed by color, nationality or any conceivable definition of race.[35]

But we can also see that we do not need a "scientific definition," that is, a definition in terms of a common biology. For

> all this has nothing to do with the plain fact that throughout the world today organized groups of men by monopoly of economic and physical power, legal enactment and intellectual training are limiting with determination and unflagging zeal the development of other groups; and that the concentration particularly of economic power today puts the majority of mankind into a slavery to the rest.[36]

And such "definitions" as he offers in *Dusk of Dawn* are not, in truth, an attempt to reflect the existing reality of race; rather, they are an attempt to call his own race to action. Du Bois moved on from the biology and the anthropology of the nineteenth century, but he never left its world of idealistic ethical nationalism.

Talk of race as a "vast family," he realized, settled little. Indeed, he was happy to entertain the thought that races were ultimately no more than hypothetical entities, with no very close correspondence to the truth. "But what is this group; and how do you differentiate it; and how can you call it 'black' when you admit it is not black?" his imagined interlocutor demands. And the rejoinder, once more is: "I recognize it quite easily and with full legal sanction: the black man is a person who must ride 'Jim Crow' in Georgia." Du Bois articulates here, in a powerful image, the core of the idea of race as an effect of social practices, as a social construction, many decades before that term became the slogan of the new cultural studies. The concept of race might be a unicorn, but its horn could draw blood.

There are moments when he revels in the Negro race, exulting over its gifts and destiny; and others when he cautions, "The race pride of Negroes is not an antidote to the race pride of white people; it is simply the other side of a hateful thing."[37] But more and more he tended to identify the black man in terms of an experience of injustice—encapsulated in the "Jim Crow" line. That trump card solved an analytic problem, but at a cost. Who would want to celebrate an artifact of injustice, one defined by an acquaintance with suffering? Who would wish for its endurance? This strain helps explains why Du Bois regularly felt obliged to ward off the inference and protest, as Garvey never needed to, that he *didn't* wish for the dissolution of the Negro—that his "one life fanaticism had been belief in my Negro blood!"[38]

Must ride "Jim Crow" in Georgia: There was the solid social fact, as unyielding as the stone Samuel Johnson kicked; to be black in America was to be a member of a subordinate caste. But what happens when the Negro becomes equated with a history of suffering? Du Bois wouldn't be the last to attempt such a move. Recall Sartre's exploration of the idea that the Jew is, in some measure, constituted by anti-Semitism. (Indeed, there is an undated jotting in the Du Bois archives: "Suddenly came the thought—are Jews black? do they know, have they suffered?")

Recall Fanon's claim that "the black soul is a white man's artifact."[39] But the tragic view of blackness as an unfortunate necessity, a dark fate, had long harried Du Bois.

In *The Souls of Black Folk,* he writes in mourning of his son, his first born, who died at age two from diphtheria: "He knew no color-line, poor dear,—and the Veil, though it shadowed him, had not yet darkened half his sun. He loved the white matron, he loved his black nurse; and in his little world walked souls alone, uncolored and unclothed. I—yea, all men—are larger and purer by the infinite breadth of that one little life." Here, little Burghardt's blessed state was never to have known race; to have been left untouched by this malign construction. ("It is wrong to introduce the child to race consciousness prematurely," Du Bois later writes.[40]) This may be race as sin, a condition of our fallen state, and the infant as without sin. Assuredly, it is race as sorrow.

There was a quasi-religious solution. One of the barely articulated themes of *Souls* is that the experience of black people in the Americas, with all its horrors, may be part of what has prepared them for their contribution to the human task. Similar chords are sounded in *Darkwater:* The "immortality of black blood" must be assured, he wrote, so that the day may come when "poverty shall be abolished, privilege be based on individual desert, and the color of a man's skin be no bar to the outlook of his soul."[41] A belief in something like divine providence—articulated perhaps as an impersonal historical force—was one element of a Victorian faith in progress, as it was central to Hegel's vision of the development of the Idea through time. It was why Du Bois could come to identify black folk in terms of a heritage of suffering and at the same time suggest, in an unavoidably Christian counterpoint, that they "are the salvation of mankind." So we alternate between the grand salvific destiny and the grim present struggle.

But, as he had long seen, there might be another way out. At the start of his career, Du Bois had spoken of a history that lay ahead, a future in which the true meaning and message of the Negro race would emerge. Yet what if the true meaning of the Negro lay in his past? Instead of defining the Negro negatively by his experience of slavery and racism—by the Middle Passage and its sequelae—perhaps the Negro could be identified by what had come before that trauma, by a deeper history. Here was a second strategy of response to the vagaries of "race." Once again,

Du Bois sought to historicize the Negro. But the task of fully historicizing the Negro—seeing the Negro not merely as an artifact of history but as a subject of history—came with a built-in challenge: What *was* the Negroes' history?

CHAPTER FOUR

The Mystic Spell

> One three centuries removed
> From the scenes his fathers loved,
>
> . . .
>
> What is Africa to me?
> —Countee Cullen, "Heritage"

THROUGHOUT his life, Du Bois sought to formulate an answer to the question that his son-in-law, Countee Cullen, asked in his best-known poem: "What is Africa to me?"[1] In his earlier years, Du Bois took Africa to be the "fount." Its history was the past that originated the narrative of the Negro. "The mystic spell of Africa is and ever was over all America," Du Bois wrote in 1908. "It has guided her hardest work, inspired her finest literature, and sung her sweetest songs. Her greatest destiny—unsensed and despised though it be,—is to give back to the first of continents the gifts which Africa of old gave to America's fathers' fathers."[2] Yet how could that origin story ever be told?

How could one go beyond the mystic spell to a real history of the Negro?

Du Bois had been raised in academic traditions that often assumed, where they did not assert, that much of Africa had no history. It is customary to trace the philosophical roots of this misapprehension to Hegel's treatment of Africa in his *Philosophy of History,* whose introduction discusses Africa in a few pages—some of them, I fear, devoted to the blood-thirsty habits of my Ashanti ancestors—and concludes famously with the remark: "At this point, we leave Africa, not to mention it again. For it is no historical part of the world; it has no movement or development to exhibit."[3]

Now you might think that Hegel, a philosopher dependent for his empirical knowledge on the work of others, was largely responding to what he could find of Africa in the missionary accounts and the travelers' tales to which he had access. In the absence of a written archive—which Ranke was to identify as the precondition for a scientific history—there was little for Hegel's contemporaries to offer up for much of the continent. This methodological prescription stood in the way of progress in African historiography until the invention of the new oral history in the 1960s. But Hegel's conclusion is not simply a reflection of the weaknesses of his sources. He reaches it in part by excluding, by a kind of fiat, the places on the African continent that he knows, from the archive, to be part of his Universal History. Carthage, he said, was a Phoenician colony and "belongs to Asia"; Egypt, likewise, "does not belong to the African Spirit." For "what we properly understand by Africa, is the Unhistorical, Undeveloped Spirit, still involved in the conditions of mere nature, and which had to be presented here only as on the threshold of the World's History."[4] If this is the proper understanding, then evidence of development is evidence that we are not dealing with the real Africa. But then we are dealing with the consequences of a definition, not with an historical discovery.

On Du Bois's account, it was Franz Boas who freed him from his dogmatic slumbers, allowing his "rather sudden awakening from the paralysis of this judgment taught me in high school and in two of the world's great universities." It happened, as Du Bois recalled, when he listened to Boas's 1906 commencement address:

Franz Boas . . . said to a graduating class: You need not be ashamed of your African past; and then he recounted the history of the black kingdoms south of the Sahara for a thousand years. I was too astonished to speak. All of this I had never heard and I came then and afterwards to realize how the silence and neglect of science can let truth utterly disappear or even be unconsciously distorted.[5]

So here was a black man, with a Harvard PhD on the history of the African slave trade and two years' social scientific training in Berlin, admitting to being astonished by the observation that Africa had a real history. For most of his countrymen, the realization would take longer still. "Few today are interested in Negro history," Du Bois wrote in 1939, "because they feel the matter already settled: the Negro has no history."[6] Even on the eve of the Second World War, this thought still had the authority of much scholarship behind it.[7]

That's not to say that Du Bois was a blank slate when it came to the topic. His first earnest discussion of Africa appeared in his 1903 study, "The Negro Church," where he ventured some anthropological observations. He began by insisting on what will now seem quite obvious: the men and women on the slave ships came with "long-formed habits of social, political, and religious life." That meant that they had their own ideas; not, perhaps, "the highest, measured by modern standards, but they were far from the lowest, measured by the standards of primitive man." He went on to discuss the organization of society into clans, remarking that they might be gathered into tribes, which might themselves be "federated into kingdoms."

> The families were polygamous, communistic groups, with one father and as many mothers as his wealth and station permitted; the family lived together in a cluster of homes, or sometimes a whole clan or village in a long, low apartment house. In such clans the idea of private property was but imperfectly developed, and never included land. The main mass of visible wealth belonged to the family and clan rather than to the individual; only in the matter of weapons and ornaments was exclusive private ownership generally recognized.

African forms of government, he went on, "varied in different tribes from absolute despotisms to limited monarchies, almost republican."[8] The "most prominent characteristic of primitive Negro religion is Nature worship with the accompanying strong belief in sorcery," but he also noted a "theistic tendency," and he quoted the authority of the *Encyclopedia Britannica,* ninth edition, for the notion that "the most widely-spread worship among Negroes and Negroids . . . is that of the moon, combined with a great veneration of the cow." (On the whole, he does better when he is not relying on *Britannica*.)

It is not the most deeply researched account, and it is largely confined to the ethnographic present. But after his "sudden awakening," Du Bois the scholar returned many times to the history of Africa, often reshaping his earlier treatments. His first major excursion came in 1915, when he published *The Negro,* the majority of which is devoted to African history. In 1930, two small volumes by Du Bois appeared in the Little Blue Book series. The first was titled *Africa: Its Geography, People and Products,* and the second was *Africa, Its Place in Modern History.* They were aimed at an African American audience thirsty for education. In the first of these pamphlets he sketched the long history of the continent; in the second, its interactions— through slavery and colonialism—with Europe and the Americas. In 1939, *Black Folk, Then and Now* appeared. It was a deeper examination of the continent's history, which borrowed (and amended) much of the material in *The Negro,* but displayed a wider grasp of Africa's modern history under European colonial rule. (Not surprisingly, I should say: much of Africa had only recently come under the control of European powers when he was writing *The Negro.* Ashanti became part of the Gold Coast colony in 1902; the sultan of Sokoto and the emir of Kano were conquered in 1903.) Du Bois undertook a third attempt at a synoptic history of Africa, *The World and Africa,* published in 1947 in the shadow of the Second World War. It begins with a chapter on "the collapse of Europe," and works back through the calamity of the slave trade to examine, through five thousand years of history, the question: "What is Africa and who are Negroes?"[9]

Africa, then, was his second front in his struggle to define the Negro. He had hoped to contribute even more to her history. As early as 1909, he planned to compose an Encyclopedia Africana that would have provided its readers with access to the latest scholarship on African history and culture in the context of the broader history of the diaspora. It was that project, now more tightly focused on Africa herself (in

part because supported by the Pan-African movement and the new nation of Ghana) that he was engaged in when he died. But that double question
"What is Africa and who are Negroes?" is the animat-
ing issue from the beginning. In the first chapter of
The Negro, more than three decades earlier, Du Bois
had written: "In this little book, then, we are study-
ing the history of the darker part of the human
family, which is separated from the rest of the human
family by no absolute physical line, but which nevertheless forms, as a mass, a social group distinct in
history, appearances, and to some extent, in spiritual gift."[10]

We have already encountered many of the elements
captured in this single sentence: the recognition of
the variability of the Negro race (implied by the absence of an "absolute physical line" distinguishing it
from the other races); the claim that Negroes are,
though not physically definable, a distinct social group,
visible in the historical record; the notion that Negroes have a distinctive contribution to make as a
group to human affairs. Yet the chapter is called "Africa," and even though the whole book places the Negro in a diasporic context (there are chapters on "The
West Indies and Latin America" and on "The Negro

in the United States") Du Bois's interest in African history plainly stems from his concern to understand the Negroes' "spiritual gift." If he could view Africa with what, in "The Conservation of Races," he had called "the eye of the historian and sociologist," he might find keys to unlocking the secret of Negro identity and, thus, a part of the answer to his unending quest to understand who he was himself.

The Negro contains a sweeping survey of black history over the very longest of longues durées, reflecting Du Bois's careful reading of the available scholarship. The published resources were somewhat limited; he had to rely on books with titles like *Negroland: or, Light Thrown upon the Dark Continent* and accounts by travelers who considered Africans to be savages and cannibals. "The time has not yet come for a complete history of the Negro peoples," he warned his readers at the start. Because he was writing before the current consensus on an African origin for our species, he locates humanity's beginnings in South Asia, out of which differentiated, he proposes, the familiar three main racial types—Mongolian, Negro, and white—to which he always retreated when he was not making finer distinctions.[11] One consequence of this picture was that he saw not just the dark-skinned people of Burma and the South Sea Islands, presumably including Australian Aborigines, as descendants of the Negro stock, but also supposed that it was Negro ancestry that "gave curly hair and a Negroid type to Jew, Syrian, and Assyrian."[12]

The survey of prehistory—it lasts only a few paragraphs—conveys the idea that on the African continent populations were shaped by a series of migrations and mixtures, including regular infusions of people from the east, through the Sinai peninsula, and from Europe, across the Mediterranean. "We find therefore, in Africa today, every degree of development in Negroid stocks and every degree of intermingling of these developments, both among African peoples and between Africans, Europeans, and Asiatics," he writes. And he continues:

The mistake is continually made of considering these types as transitions between absolute Caucasians and absolute Negroes. No such absolute type ever existed on either side. Both were slowly differentiated from a common ancestry and continually remingled their blood. . . . From prehistoric times down to to-day Africa is, in this sense, primarily the land of the mulatto. So, too, was earlier

Europe and Asia; only in these countries the mulatto was early bleached by climate, while in Africa he was darkened.[13]

This mixed population produces the major cultural zones whose history he will sketch in the chapters that follow, beginning with Ethiopia and Egypt, the cultures of the Nile—"probably the first of higher human cultures," Du Bois says. (The Egyptians, he says, "were what would be described in America as a light mulatto stock of Octoroons or Quadroons.") Then we pass in quick succession through the cultures of the Sudan; the people who eventually made Zimbabwe; the Bantu; the Phoenician, Greek, and Roman colonies of North Africa; Carthage; Benin and the Yoruba-speaking peoples. Islam makes its arrival: "Beginning in the tenth century and slowly creeping across the desert into Negroland, the new religion found an already existent culture and came, not as a conqueror, but as an adapter and inspirer. Civilization received new impetus and a wave of Mohammedanism swept eastward, erecting the great kingdoms of Melle, the Songhay, Bornu, and the Hausa states"—a "splendid history of civilization and uplift."[14]

When he works up to the rise of the Atlantic slave economy, beginning in the fifteenth century, Du Bois stresses that slavery, in Africa as elsewhere, does not begin as racial slavery: it began "to center in Africa," he says, "for religious and political rather than for racial reasons."[15] A slave trade in Africans, he contends, was made possible by the weakness of African states (he had suggested as much back in 1903); Africa's peoples lived typically in a "culture of family town and small tribe." "Only the integrating force of state building could have stopped this slave trade," he writes. He argues that two great waves of state building—in Ethiopia, in Southern Africa—failed under pressure from Egypt, Persia, Rome, and Byzantium (in the case of Ethiopia) and the "Bantu hordes" (in the case of South Africa); and then goes on to suggest that, because the states of the Gulf of Guinea (Benin, Yoruba) "never got much beyond a federation of large industrial cities," they, too, were unable to resist the inroads of slavers from elsewhere. Only in the western Sudan, under the influence of Islam, did large empires survive. And these were destroyed, first, by resistance from the "heathen south," second by the closing off of the trade to the Mediterranean "by the Moors in the sixteenth century."[16] These pressures disrupted the states of West Africa, leaving them open to predation by the European traders who arrived on the coast of Guinea in growing numbers, increasingly insistently demanding slaves, in the succeeding centuries.

Du Bois ends this summary chapter with a catalog of disasters that followed:

> Under such circumstances there could be but one end: the virtual uprooting of ancient African culture, leaving only misty reminders of the ruin in the customs and work of the people. To complete the disaster came the partition of the continent among European nations and the modern attempt to exploit the country and natives for the economic benefit of the white world, together with the transplanting of black nations to the new western world and their rise in self-assertion there.

In a typical passage in the later chapters, Du Bois discusses the rise and fall of empires that Boas had first drawn to his attention. We hear of the Pharaoh Necho II of Egypt, who, according to Herodotus, had sent Phoenician sailors on a successful circumnavigation of the continent;[17] and of Hanno, from Carthage, who sailed down Africa's western shoreline.[18] We learn of the mediaeval kingdom of Ghana, rich with gold, whose kings could trace their ancestry back through twenty-one generations and seventy-four rulers back to 700 BCE.

These passages contain, in their details, much for a modern historian to dispute. One might question such ethical assumptions as that Africans (unlike Europeans and Asians) would have avoided selling their continental brethren into slavery if they could have; or the methodological assumption that king lists, on their own, provide a reliable guide to chronology. But what is striking, I think, is how many of the places and peoples he mentions would figure in a contemporary accounting of the history of the continent. Du Bois gives a compelling account of the broad sweep of regional history, insisting on the central place not just of warfare but also of commerce in the spread of culture and the growth of power.

What is equally striking, though, is that this is apologetic history, in the strict sense: it is the rational defense, through historical argument, of a position. And the position is the cultural nationalism that he had adopted long ago: that "the Negro people, as a race, have a contribution to make to civilization and humanity, which no other race can make." His intellectual task is to clear away misconceptions about Africa's people and their descendants: to confirm Boas's claim that black people "need not be ashamed of [their] African past."

Past Imperfect

Appearing a quarter century later, *Black Folk, Then and Now* is a fuller work. While it draws a good deal on the elements of the earlier work, it also shows his constant absorption of new scholarly ideas. Now, for example, he tells us, "It may well be that Africa rather than Asia was the birthplace of the human family and ancient Negro blood the basis of the blood of all men."[19] So Du Bois's readers will have been among the first to hear of the new consensus on an African origin for our species. One larger difference between the two accounts is the elaboration of details about the variety of cultural and demographic zones in the continent, which reflects the approach of the 1930s pamphlet on African geography. Here, Du Bois sees in the disposition of rivers and harbors, lowlands and highlands, forests, deserts, and savannas an environment that shapes the historical possibilities of the continent's inhabitants; and those claims, which echo the eighteenth- and nineteenth-century natural historians and geographers, have been resurrected in our own day by economists like Jeffrey Sachs.[20]

Black Folk, Then and Now is also a darker book. It features a much more detailed and extensive engagement with contemporary history and, in particular, with the issues facing black people in colonial Africa. So, for example, Du Bois has a fascinating discussion (in a chapter on "The Land in Africa") of differences in colonial policy in relation to land tenure. He distinguishes clearly between the settler regimes of East and Southern Africa and the French and British colonies in tropical West Africa—both areas where little European settlement took place—and the barbarous regime in the Belgian Congo. And he combines an analysis of the differences in the pattern of the alienation of land with reflections on different labor regimes (especially in the chapter "The African Laborer") in a way that anticipates a comparative history of the political economies of colonial Africa that is still to be written.

Throughout the book one sees Du Bois's method at work: his sociologist's imagination, exploring the ways economic relations and other social forces drive and are driven by ideologies; his historian's concern for the etiology of contemporary arrangements; his pragmatist's interest in connecting analysis with solutions. And while his language is often socialist, and he makes free allusions to Marx, the discussion is always inflected by the independent significance of race alongside—often above—class.

All this is evident in the peroration on the book's last page: "There was a time when poverty was due mainly to scarcity, but today it is due to monopoly founded on our industrial organization. This strangle hold must be broken." So far, then, a routine socialist sociological analysis. But the solution Du Bois offers in the next few lines is expressed in a language that resonates strongly with the romantic traditions with which I began. For he tells us that this stranglehold will be broken "not so much by violence and revolution, which is only the outward distortion of an inner fact, but by the ancient cardinal virtues: individual prudence, courage, temperance, and justice, and the more modern faith, hope and love." Standing arrayed against these cardinal virtues is "the blind and insane will to mass murder which is the dying spasm of that decadent exploitation of human labor as a commodity, born of the Negro slave trade"—an exploitation grounded in "the persistent disbelief in the ability and desert of the vast majority of men."[21]

Here, then, alongside the expression of his faith in the potential of individual agency, is a theory of the historical sources of the ideology that sustains exploitation. But at the end, we return to the issue of race, understood now clearly as the product of social forces, of ideologies and economic relations.

> The proletariat of the world consists not simply of white European and American workers but overwhelmingly of the dark workers of Asia, Africa, the islands of the sea, and South and Central America. These are the ones who are supporting a superstructure of wealth, luxury, and extravagance. It is the rise of these people that is the rise of the world. The problem of the twentieth century is the problem of the color line.[22]

You will recall that this was something he had now been saying for nearly forty years. If there is an unhelpful conflation of issues here—of race and class, of colonial and metropolitan relations of production— the book certainly supports Du Bois's claim that understanding race is one of the keys to unlocking the central moral and political questions of his time. The twentieth century can sort itself out, Du Bois suggests, only if it sorts out the question that had followed him from the very beginnings: "What is the real meaning of Race?"

But perhaps the question could not be finally sorted out, only repeated and reformulated. In *The World and Africa* Du Bois argues, once more, that the slave trade "is the prime and effective cause of the contradictions in European civilization and the illogic in modern thought and the collapse of human culture."[23] Much of the rest of the book follows the same course as the earlier ones, again capturing new detail and new causes for sorrow or outrage. And, as usual, he ends the last complete chapter with a cosmopolitan peroration:

> The fire and freedom of black Africa, with the uncurbed might of her consort Asia, are indispensable to the fertilizing of the universal soil of mankind, which Europe alone never would or could give this aching earth.[24]

Long after the ascendancy of the Rankeans, Du Bois remained an adherent of the ancient adage that history is philosophy learned from examples.[25]

What, then, was Africa to him? A harrowed, ravished land. But not only. It was, at times, a loamy, primordial bastion of the communal spirit, a magical realm of lotus eaters. In 1923, shortly after writing up his caustic definition of the black person as one who "must ride 'Jim Crow' in Georgia," Du Bois made his first trip to Africa. He found it magical. "The spell of Africa is upon me," he wrote. "The ancient witchery of her medicine is burning in my drowsy, dreamy blood." He swelled to the chords of romantic primitivism—the scholar of Africa he admired most was Leo Frobenius—and broke into rapturous effusions about the land and its people.[26] He was enthralled by the Africans' "laziness; divine, eternal, languor is right and good and true," and stirred by "their intertwined communal souls," their gift for "sinking the individual in the social." A homecoming? *Es war so schön gewesen. Es hat nicht sollen sein.*[27] However adoring the language, this most industrious of men, this quarrelsome, heroic individualist, was gazing upon the not-I.

The not-I never called him out as such, though. For, in another respect, what made Africa so intoxicating was the same thing that had made Germany so intoxicating: it was a land where he was not seen, or not seen primarily, as a Negro—a land where his racial identity lost its salience. "Here darkness descends and rests on lovely skins until brown seems luscious and natural," he wrote. Brown bodies as far as the eye could see! Du Bois, raised in the largely white world of Great Barrington, was a man for whom race consciousness was, in the first instance, the result of being seen as a Negro by someone who wasn't. (It is the sense captured in Fanon's recollection of a white child crying, "Mummy, look, a Negro, I'm scared!") The black institutions he built were essentially outward-facing, batteries meant to repel white racism. For him, there's a sense in which Africa, far from being Negroland, was the land of no Negroes.

Either way, if he hoped to learn about himself by learning about Africa—by a profound immersion in its cultures and history—the result was paradoxical. By installments, his studies of Africa served to complicate rather than clarify his sense of the Negro.

It some ways, to be sure, it replenished it, just as he had hoped. There is pride taken in a glorious past of brown pharaohs and golden pyramids; but Du Bois, despite his fascination with "Negroid" features on Egyptian statues, does not make the full "Afrocentric" turn. He evoked the feudal majesty of gold-amassing medieval empires; but his deepening Marxism limited their allure for him. And always the slave trade—the "heart disease of Africa"—cast its long shadow, as did the subsequent history of colonial conquest and subjugation. Calamity bulks larger in each of his histories. "The partition, domination, and exploitation of Africa gradually entered my thought as part of my problem of race," he recalled, and the specter of the racialized ideology of Empire haunted him: "the white race as ruler of all the world, and the world working for it, and the world's wealth piled up for the white man's gain," a "white world which is today dominating human culture and working for the continued subordination of the colored races." He globalized his earlier, bitter formula about the Negro being the person who rode Jim Crow in Georgia. Now the Negro was imbricated in larger, global systems of injustice; he could be defined by his victimization at the hands of "industrial imperialism." And so Du Bois's "color-line" warnings from 1900 become the basis of a new definition.

Take another look at Du Bois's early proposal that a race was a vast family sharing the same impulses, traditions, and strivings for ideals of life. Could such impulses, traditions, and ideals really have been shared by most Negroes over the ages, from the Zambezi plain to a Harlem ballroom? That seems to be the thesis. But another, against-the-grain reading is also possible. The sentence could express the claim that the Negro came into existence only once those conditions were met—once it had become, in the Hegelian formula, a group in itself and for itself. (In itself: defined by a relation to "white imperial industry" marked by exclusion, oppression, and exploitation. For itself: mindful of its identity and its interests and in pursuit of them.)

In *Dusk of Dawn,* Du Bois wonders again what Africa is to him. Was it the history of a race? Once, he says, it would have been his ready response; now the concept seems a morass of contradiction. "But one thing is sure and that is the fact that since the fifteenth century these ancestors of mine and their other descendants have had a common history; have suffered a common disaster and have one long memory," he writes. "The physical bond is least and the badge of color relatively unimportant save as a badge; the real essence of his kinship is its social heritage of slavery, the discrimination and insult; and this heritage binds together not simply the children of Africa but extends through yellow Asia and into the South Seas.

It is this unity that draws me to Africa." A unity, a heritage, that is now avowedly trans-racial and no longer a sweet gift of the racial spirit but a grueling genealogy of oppression. In that reading, the Negro is anything but ancient, and, once more, the end of blackness is devoutly to be wished.[28]

There is a simple, startling line in *Dusk of Dawn,* and it follows a recounting of his 1923 African raptures: "Now to return to the American concept of race."[29] *The American concept.* The taproot has snapped. Race was not what ties him to the land of his dark ancestors; it was merely an "American concept." In moments like these, Africa isn't filling in the idea of the Negro so much as marking its limits. The "mystic spell" had been broken.

CHAPTER FIVE

The One and the Many

> This was the race concept which has dominated my
> life. . . . Perhaps it is wrong to speak of it at all
> as "a concept," rather than as a group of
> contradictory forces, facts, and tendencies.
> —W. E. B. Du Bois, *Dusk of Dawn*

In an essay on his "evolving program for Negro free-dom," Du Bois describes a disciplinary crisis that be-fell him when he was in his forties. "Facts, in social science, I realized, were elusive things: emotions, loves, hates, were facts; and they were facts in the souls and minds of the scientific student, as well as in the persons studied," he wrote. "Their measurement, then, was doubly difficult and intricate." In investigating the 1917 race riot in East St. Louis, Du Bois says, he realized that any recounting merely of the "cold, bare facts of history" would omit too much; and then there were the limitations on what facts he could actually uncover. Any story he could tell would be "woefully incomplete." His Berlin mentors in the social sciences had taught him to sift through the data for provisional patterns and laws. This no longer sat well with Du Bois. He asked himself what law he was seeking, what law governed the "world of interracial discord" around him.

> I fell back upon my Royce and James and deserted Schmoller and Weber. I saw the action of physical law in the actions of men; but I saw more than that: I saw rhythms and tendencies; coincidences and probabilities; and I saw that, which for want of any other word, I must in accord with the strict tenets of Science, call Chance. I went forward to build a sociology, which I conceived of as the attempt to measure the element of Chance in human conduct. This was the Jamesian pragmatism, applied not simply to ethics, but to all human action, beyond what seemed to me, increasingly, the distinct limits of physical law.[1]

By "chance" he meant not mere contingency but *volition*—the human factor. In the sway of this disciplinary crisis, as we've seen, Du Bois increasingly dematerializes, de-reifies, race. He had long recognized the color line as a global phenomenon, and so he had turned to Africa as a means of reconstructing his "race identity," looking for a way to make it something grander than an artifact of racism and injustice. A familiar limitation to so-called identity politics, one to which Marxists have been especially attuned, is that the condition of being impoverished or oppressed isn't a comfortable basis of a self-affirmative identity, given that this very condition is what the politics seeks to abolish. ("Pauper Pride" isn't a slogan for uplift.) If the Negro really was one who must ride Jim Crow in Georgia, Du Bois sought, in a sense, to abolish the Negro. Africa promised an alternate conception. But, as we saw, it only underscored the message of his sorrow songs; there too oppression defined identity. Color remained an index of injustice. Meanwhile, an empirical sociology of structure failed to deliver explanation, understanding, or advancement. Where did that leave him?

In the combined forces of James and Royce, he found a body of argument attuned to the nonrational wellsprings of human behavior and another attuned to the collective dimension of human purpose and strivings. To make sense of the role that race had played in human affairs, he later wrote, we had to survey the "vague and uncharted lands" that are the

subconscious drivers of most of our actions, a James-
ian realm of "conditioned reflexes; of long followed
habits, customs and folkways; of subconscious trains
of reasoning and unconscious nervous reflexes."[2] This
was to be coupled with the Roycean emphasis upon
the ways that human loyalties draw from and create
communities of meaning.[3]

Du Bois liked to talk about the "long memory"
that might bind Negroes together *as* Negroes. Could
such a collective memory do the work Du Bois hoped
it would? Hadn't Renan declared history—real history, truth told about the past—the enemy of the nation, precisely because the nation subsisted on fable
and forgetting, as well as on the reality of a remembered past? ("L'oubli, et je dirai même l'erreur histo-
rique, sont un facteur essentiel de la création d'une
nation." Forgetting, I would even say historical error,
is an essential factor in the creation of a nation.) Bene-
dict Anderson was to term the nation an "imagined
community," but you hardly need to be nation-sized
for that term to apply. Once "community" means more
than you, me, and everyone we know, it's a construct
that is bound to draw upon the imaginings of its
members. Here, Royce offered support. He defined a
"community of memory," one that was "constituted

by the fact that each of its members accepts as a part of his own individual life and self the same *past* events that each of his fellow-members accepts." And, similarly, communities may be brought together by a shared projection of the future: a community in which "each of its members accepts, as part of his own individual life and self, the same expected *future* events that each of his fellows accepts, may be called a *community of expectation* or . . . a *community of hope*."[4]

In the conjunction of James and Royce, two amiable sparring partners, you had the former's appreciation of the contingency of social forms and the latter's sense of their power, value, and even necessity. You had the pragmatist's suspicion of the "natural" and the idealist's sense of how purpose arose in community. In the crossroads, Du Bois could locate his own project. In particular, he could glimpse a strategy that sidestepped certain of his difficulties and brought him close to a notion of race as what we'd now call a social identity.

Identity Now

There are four crucial dimensions to the contemporary philosophical theory of identity. (The formulation is my own, but I take it to capture a widely shared understanding.) First, social identities—this is an insight from labeling theory in sociology—depend for their existence on there being labels for them. This is because people respond to others and think of themselves by way of these labels: we think of people as Caucasians or Canadians or Catholics and then respond to them as such; we think of ourselves as Americans and do (or don't do) things because that is what we think we are. So the first point is metaphysical: nominalism about social identities is preferable to ontological realism. What holds groups together is often not a shared essence but simply a shared name. The first point, then, in a slogan, is that *social identities require labels*.

Social-identity labels are often contested at the boundaries: we have no consensus as to whether the daughter of an African-American and an Aleut, raised in Alaska, is "really black," or the son of an African and a Native Hawaiian is "really Hawaiian." These are the sorts of things we must accept there can be endless argument about, even if those engaged in these arguments may not regard them with this sort of ironic distance. The contestability of the boundaries is, by the way, the main reason why philosophical nominalism seems like the only view about identities that will do. To say that the boundaries are contestable isn't to say there are no clear cases. If, once the evidence is in, you judge that Barack Obama isn't a man and Denzel Washington isn't an African-American, we will have lost our semantic bearings altogether: there can be clear answers to questions about the ascription of concepts with fuzzy edges. This acknowledged contestability, built into our use of the terms, is suggestively like the essential contestability of many normative concepts, which W. B. Gallie pointed to years ago.[5]

And indeed, the second dimension of identity that I want to point to is precisely that there are *norms* associated with social identities: *norms of identification,* as we might call them, which specify ways that people of a certain identity ought to behave; and *norms of treatment,* ways that people of a certain identity ought or ought not to be responded to and acted upon. (We can report the norms indifferently as saying what people ought and ought not and what they should and should not do.) My shorthand for this second claim is that *identity is normative.*

These "shoulds" and "oughts" need not be especially glorious; nor need they be specifically moral. It is a philosopher's mistake to forget that "oughts" and "shoulds" are not the special property of morality. That men shouldn't wear skirts isn't a moral truth; indeed, I don't think it's a truth at all. Nevertheless, we live in a society in which there is a norm to this effect: people don't just expect men not to wear skirts, they expect them not to do so *because* they recognize that men ought not to do so. We expect men not to wear skirts because we know they think they shouldn't (or, at the very least, they don't think they should). It's not the mere rarity of the man in skirts that generates this prediction. But the norms (like the criteria of membership) are not usually agreed to by all—there are those cross-dressing men—and there are often interesting disputes about them. It is part of our understanding of these norms, then, that they too are contestable.

Here are some more examples of the type of norm I have in mind. Negatively: blacks ought not to embarrass their race; Jews and Muslims ought not to eat pork. Positively: gay people ought to come out; blacks ought to support affirmative action. To say that these norms exist isn't to endorse them; I could not give full-hearted assent to any of these norms. The existence of a norm that people of some kind ought to do something amounts only to its being widely thought—and widely known to be thought—that they ought to do it.

The third dimension of identity flows from the second. Because there are norms of identification, people who identify through the labels *as X, act* sometimes *as Xs;* by which I mean that one reason they act as they do is that they are motivated by the thought, "I've a reason to do *A* because I am an *X*."

This last point makes explicit the fact that we now see *identities as centrally subjective,* in the sense that their importance derives from the role they play in the conscious thoughts and acts of those who bear them. So identities, we now think, are *nominal, normative, and subjective:* all of these being features, of course, that may explain why we routinely speak of them nowadays as socially constructed.

That the identities I am talking about are subjective in this way is a key part of the view. We pick out the subjective identities because they have a crucial role in something quite specific—and this is the fourth element of the account—namely the making of our lives. Norms of identification are central in the project of individuality, which is the creation of a distinctive human life.

A very wide range of kinds of people fit the general rubric I have laid out. Our modern story of identity answers the question of what the things "like" race and gender and sexual orientation and nationality and religion are; what it meant to say "nationality and religion, *and suchlike things.*" They are the nominal, normative, subjective classifications of persons. We can now add, for example, professional identities: teacher, critic, philosopher; vocations: artist, composer, novelist; affiliations, formal and informal: baseball fan, jazz aficionado, blues man; and other more airy labels: dandy, intellectual, cosmopolitan.

Identity before "Identity"

Once again, this theory arises from an intellectual matrix that will, I think, reward a little scrutiny. It will help if we're not bound to the specific language of "identity"; as Quentin Skinner has famously argued, the history of concepts is not necessarily a history of their names. "Identity" didn't acquire its contemporary valence until the fifties and sixties.[6] But was the notion beyond conceiving in Du Bois's day? Let's take a look at the matrix for such inquiry, in the 1890s and after.

Consider Williams James's claim, in *The Principles of Psychology* (1890), that a person has "as many different social selves as there are distinct groups of persons about whose opinion he cares."[7] What's the nature of those "social selves?" According to James,

> Nothing is commoner than to hear people discriminate between their different selves of this sort: "As a man I pity you, but as an official I must show you no mercy; as a politician I regard him as an ally, but as a moralist I loathe him;" etc., etc. What may be called "club-opinion" is one of the very strongest forces in life.[8]

He goes on to explore the notion of the "potential social self": defined through the others to whom I appeal when I defect from an identity group—convert from Protestantism to Catholicism, say. The social judges in question may not even be alive; maybe it's the future generations whose approval I seek.[9] Here, in discussing the social self, James inches toward Royce, whose "philosophy of loyalty"—in which individuality gained meaning from its enmeshment in a larger cause, so long as it was socially binding, and ethically just—also entrained a sort of philosophy of identity.

An even fuller account of identity, *avant la lettre,* was advanced by George Herbert Mead. I said at the start that if we want to know what ideas were "in the air," we can learn much from Du Bois's fellow students, whether or not they were rubbing elbows. One person I had in mind was Mead, who, like Du Bois, was born in small-town Massachusetts; he studied (with Royce and James) at Harvard from 1887–1888, just missing Du Bois, and later at the University of Berlin (1889–1891, where he was a pupil of Dilthey's), again just missing Du Bois. If we want to know what conceptual apparatus was available with respect to what we now call identity—if we want to know what tools were at hand to think about the relations between individuality and collective identity—we cannot ignore Mead, who was preoccupied with these issues. He was part of the matrix (a term he himself had some fondness for); he drew from it and contributed to it.[10]

Mead, five years older than Du Bois, is now taken as a founder of what later was called "symbolic interactionism," close kin to labeling theory. "The full development of the individual's self," Mead argued, "is constituted not only by an organization of these particular individual attitudes, but also by an organization of the social attitudes of the generalized other or the social group as a whole to which he belongs." The term "generalized other" can be misunderstood: it referred not to some lurking nicht-Ich but to "the organized community or social group which gives to the individual his unity of self." (Mead also used the term "significant others.") For a ball player, to take Mead's example, the generalized other was the team. And what he wanted us to understand was that the mind "is essentially a social phenomenon." Mead thought that social institutions "are not necessarily subversive of individuality in the individual members." He saw no reason that such institutions shouldn't be "flexible and progressive, fostering individuality rather than discouraging it."[11]

This talk of the "unity" of self could make it sound as if Mead, unlike James, didn't take on board the multiple nature of (what we now call) identity. He did.

We carry on a whole series of different relationships to different people. We are one thing to one man and another thing to another. There are parts of the self which exist only for the self in relationship to itself. We divide ourselves up in all sorts of different selves with reference to our acquaintances.

We discuss politics with one and religion with another. There are all sorts of different selves an-
swering to all sorts of different social reactions. It
is the social process itself that is responsible for the
appearance of the self; it is not there as a self apart
from this type of experience. A multiple personality is in a certain sense normal.[12]

Mead's famous distinction between the "I" and
the "me" corresponds, in a very rough sort of way, to
the distinction between your *individuality* and your
identity. "The 'I' is the response of the organism to
the attitudes of the others; the 'me' is the organized
set of attitudes of others which one himself assumes,"
Mead says. "The attitudes of the others constitute
the organized 'me,' and then one reacts toward that
as an 'I.'"[13]

Like his teacher Royce, Mead worried about insu-
larity: "We all belong to small cliques, and we may
remain simply inside them. The 'organized other' present in ourselves is then a community of a narrow diam-
eter. We are struggling now to get a certain amount of
international-mindedness. We are realizing ourselves
as members of a larger community."[14] Royce had said
something similar in the *Philosophy of Loyalty*: "For

where the special loyalties are, amongst our people, most developed, they far too often take the form of a loyalty to mutually hostile partisan organizations, or to sects, or to social classes, at the expense of loyalty to the community or to the whole country."[15] Like Du Bois, they hoped that identities could be reformed; that they could be made more cosmopolitan and less insular.

So here was the matrix of something very like modern identity theory. Much of Du Bois's own thought looks aligned with it. Indeed, this conceptual field brings together points that Du Bois was among the first to make clearly about one social identity: that of the Negro. We can begin with Du Bois's recognition that race—as a species of social identity—is made in and through social processes. "It is strange what small things determine the course of human lives," he wrote in a marveling mood. "My life, for instance, has been conditioned by the color of my skin. This fact, trivial of itself, was of cosmic importance in the eyes of the world at the time I was born." He grasped how something inherently arbitrary could acquire vast significance. Lotze may have promoted suspicion about natural kinds; Dilthey would have encouraged a sense of every category's historical contingency. But

Du Bois was not alone among his American peers in thinking that gleaming theory might gain from being scuffed up by reality. As for the label "Negro," Du Bois granted that the term "is not 'historically' accurate." On the other hand, what name was?

> Neither "English," "French," "German," "White," "Jew," "Nordic" nor "Anglo-Saxon." They were all at first nicknames, misnomers, accidents, grown eventually to conventional habits and achieving accuracy because, and simply because, wide and continued usage rendered them accurate.[16]

So conventions could spawn realities. In identifying the key role of the "badge," as he put it, of hair and color—the key role of such placards for the racial label "Negro"—Du Bois's social constructionism is precisely a kind of nominalism. It is a nominalism that urges us to move from thinking of the Negro race as a natural, biological kind to thinking of it as composed of people who share a socially made identity. I don't think Du Bois ever fully made this move: until the end of his life he spoke of the Negro as a category that worked across societies, in ways that seem to ignore his own insight. But his work encourages us, in the end, to make this move without him. Du Bois liked to imagine himself, as he wrote in *Souls,* as a Moses "standing upon this high Pigsah," as "I sight the promised land."[17] Perhaps we can leave him behind us in the realism of Moab, while we travel to the promised land of nominalism.

Du Bois certainly helps us see that the ethical significance of our identities derives from the way those identities give us projects; from the fact that, as he put in his Negro Creed more than a century ago, people of a shared identity strive "together for the accomplishment of certain more of less vividly conceived ideals of life." We can see with him, too, that the meaning of an identity is determined not only by the bearers of the badge, but also by the responses of others: that "the black man is a person who must ride 'Jim Crow' in Georgia." He did not suppose that the group had an independent character apart from these norms and practices. Indeed, in *Dusk of Dawn,* he affirms "the group"—taken as an entity "which had action, guilt, praise, and blame quite apart from the persons composing the group"—to be merely a sociologist's hypothesis; as he says, perhaps wistfully, "no such group over-soul has been proven to exist."[18] And he understood, as we do, that people can have many identities—and that one of them might be a cosmopolitan identity as human beings, citizens of a shared world.

The identity concept enables a certain agnosticism about history. It wears its provisionality on its face, curling up like Du Bois's *kaiserlich* mustache. But it is open to history, and, especially, to the historical narratives through which communities understand themselves. As we've seen, Du Bois saw that Negro identity, like American identity, need be rooted neither in blood nor in a shared character; it could be situated in a place and an identification with its history. Africa was the home of the Negro, not just in the sense that that was where black people originally came from, but in the sense that stories of Africa's past—African history—might figure in the subjective life of self-consciously black people. Once he understood the Negro sociohistorically, the significance of African descent didn't need to lie in the genes that African-Americans brought from Africa; it could lie in cultural traditions or in the continuing significance of a black identity in the world. Inasmuch as black people share a black identity and that identity is narratively rooted in Africa, what happens in and to Africa affects black people everywhere: through their own identifications as well as through the views of others.

Just as American patriots live their identity through stories of America—stories rooted, sometimes rather loosely, in the soil of historical fact—so a black identity engages you with tales of an African past. And it is no barrier to full engagement with those narratives to discover that your own particular ancestors were elsewhere when the events they record occurred. Told right, such stories *do* bind people together so that they can accomplish shared goals. This point—it is Ernest Renan's famous insight about the connection between historical narratives and nationalism—is one on which Du Bois relied on the many occasions he sought to rally black people to the cause of black liberation.[19]

Go Down, Moses

So Du Bois found his way into a narrowing orbit around a notion of race that was nominalist, narrative, subjective, normative, and even, sometimes, antirealist. Why wasn't this enough? Why did the subject continue to vex him so profoundly? And plainly it did: he never felt that he had mastered the concept; if anything, he felt undone by it. "Thus in my life the chief fact has been race," he writes in *Dusk of Dawn*. "Yet how shall I explain and clarify its meaning for a soul? Description fails." The race concept vexed him with "illogical trends and irreconcilable tendencies," and he wondered further: "Perhaps it is wrong to speak of it at all as 'a concept' rather than as a group of contradictory forces, facts and tendencies."[20] He could qualify, define, and redefine, but he could not quite gain the upper hand. It was the angel he wrestled with his entire life.

At the start of his career, he spoke of the message for the world that would one day unfold; toward the end of his life, he moved from the language of striving to that of struggle, from *streben* to *kampfen,* and sometimes thought he found that message in the global gearings of class warfare. Often, he supposed that Pan-Africanism could provide a new, global vanguard. Sometimes he thought the key to uplift was to be found in a supra-racial communion of shared struggle. The generality of the identity schema is its strength—and its weakness. Du Bois needed an idea that would unite the dark masses and inspire their strivings, and a naked account of social identity wasn't adequate to the task. Identity theory is an account from outside, an explanation without true understanding.

It wasn't that political potency required self-deception. But it did entail, for Du Bois, some mystic spell of a shared memory and a pulsing sense of a common destiny; and he couldn't find a theoretical account that rationally supported what he felt. Enlightenment and counter-Enlightenment contended in the breast of one man. It is what makes Du Bois a romantic. It's why he continually reached for a religious, a providential, language, even as he chastened himself for it. "Our whole basis of knowledge is so relative and contingent," he worried, that we got nowhere when we tried to argue about "ultimate reality and the real essence of life and the past and the future."[21] Yet what choice was there? Du Bois would say that the race concept should be retained, or that a black identity should be preserved, until justice and freedom reigns on earth. But here, once more, we move from sociology to soteriology: insofar as blackness contains the seeds for that blessed state, it strives, ultimately, for its own disappearance.

Starting in his middle years, a fateful air hovers over Du Bois's work. He had decided that the task of social uplift would be even harder, slower than he'd once imagined. Yet he never gave up his own belief in progress as an unfurling law of historical development.

Shortly before he turned ninety—and five years before he sent off that telegram to the marchers at Washington—Du Bois composed a "Last Message to the World." He said he looked forward to the "long, deep and endless sleep," and the handing on of his tasks for others to complete. He concluded:

> One thing alone I charge you. As you live, believe in life! Always human beings will live and progress to greater, broader and fuller life.
>
> The only possible death is to lose belief in this truth simply because the great end comes slowly, because time is long.[22]

If he could no longer imagine that racial inequality would be much lessened within his lifetime, he believed in a kind of providence at the end, as he had at the start. He was sure, like Martin Luther King Jr., that however long the arc of the moral universe, it did bend toward justice. And yet the more exalted his talk of universal brotherhood and sisterhood, the more his struggle could sound like a lost cause. He may sometimes have imagined that it was. Still, he knew from a long life the truth he would have read in his old teacher Josiah Royce: that "loyalty to lost causes is one of the most potent influences of human history."

It was "attended," Royce wrote, "by two comrades, grief and imagination," and energized by them.[23] It was the whole history of the Christian church; it could turn small tribes into great nations; it could turn great nations into greater ones. This Du Bois understood, too, and never more so than when the marchers prepared for their protest in the National Mall. The Ghanaian from Great Barrington, who was so often drawn to the figure of Moses, knew now that he would die in the wilderness. He sent off his telegram to the future, went to sleep, and did not awake. He never lived to see the day the country of his birth would truly imagine blackness as something other than a badge of "discrimination and insult." But he helped usher in the dusk of that dawn.

NOTES

INTRODUCTION

1. See http://www.hu-berlin.de/pr/medien/publikationen
   /pdf/feuerbach_en, accessed July 10, 2013; and W. E. B. Du
   Bois, *The Autobiography of W. E. B. Du Bois* (New York:
   Oxford University Press, 2007; originally published in
   1968), p. 12 (hereafter *Autobiography*).

2. In *Autobiography*, p. 12, Du Bois notes, "I had coveted this
   degree 64 years before," although he mistakenly makes
   the year 1959. Hamilton Beck suggests that the awarding
   of the degree was a hurried affair; and recounts the
   East Germans' efforts to discourage Du Bois from visit-
   ing his old lodgings in the West. See his "Censoring Your
   Ally: W. E. B. Du Bois in the GDR," in David McBride,
   Leroy Hopkins, and Carol Aisha Blackshire-Belay, eds.,
   *Crosscurrents—African-Americans, Africa, and Germany
   in the Modern Age* (Columbia, SC: Camden House, 1998),
   pp. 197–219; and Shirley Graham Du Bois, *His Day Is
   Marching On: A Memoir of W. E. B. Du Bois* (Philadelphia:
   Lippincott, 1971), p. 256. Sieglinde Lemke reproduces actual texts of the ceremony from the Humboldt archives;
   see her invaluable "Berlin and Boundaries: *Sollen* versus
   geschehen," *boundary 2* 27, no. 3 (Fall 2000): 45–78 (hereafter "Berlin"). I have modified her translation on the basis
   of the German text she reproduces: "Lernen, Forschen,
   Lehren und Kämpfen für die Anwendung des Erkannten—
   das kennzeichnet die vielen Jahrzehnte Ihres Wirkens . . .

Voll Bewunderung und Ehrfurcht, hochverehrter Professor Du Bois, erkennen wir die einzigartige Synthese zwischen Wissenschaft und politisch-gestaltendem Handeln, die ihr ganzes Leben auszeichnet. Der Rat meiner Fakultät hat daher einstimmig beschlossen, Ihnen für ihre hohe wissenschaftliche Leistung, sowie für Ihren einzigartigen Verdienst im Befreiungskampf der Neger innerhalb und ausserhalb der USA und für Ihren so tapferen Einsatz zur Erhaltung des Friedens den Doktor der Wirtschaftswissenschaften ehrenhalber zu verleihen." "Berlin," p. 76, fn. 66. (Translations are mine unless otherwise indicated.)

3. W. E. B. Du Bois, "My Evolving Program for Negro Freedom," in Rayford W. Logan, ed., *What the Negro Wants* (Chapel Hill: University of North Carolina Press, 1944), p. 38 (hereafter "Evolving Program").

4. See Kwame Anthony Appiah, "Building Post Roads of the New Millennium," University of Pennsylvania Baccalaureate Address, 2007, http://www.upenn.edu/almanac/volumes/v53/n34/c-bac-ka.html, accessed July 10, 2013.

5. See Robert K. Merton, "Singletons and Multiples in Scientific Discovery: A Chapter in the Sociology of Science," *Proceedings of the American Philosophical Society* 105, no. 5, The Influence of Science upon Modern Culture, Conference Commemorating the 400th Anniversary of the Birth of Francis Bacon (October 13, 1961): 470–486.

6. "The Age of Miracles began with Fisk and ended with Germany," in W. E. B. Du Bois, *Darkwater: Voices from within the Veil* (New York: Oxford University Press, 2007; originally published in 1920), p. 7 (hereafter *Darkwater*). Lyman Abbott's claim is from "Remarks by Dr. Lyman Abbott," in *First Mohonk Conference on the Negro Question*

(Boston: George Ellis, 1890), p. 82 et seq. Du Bois's description of Douglass appears in chapter 3 of W. E. B. Du Bois, *The Souls of Black Folk* (New York: Oxford University Press, 2007; originally published in 1903), pp. 24–25 (hereafter *Souls*).

7. *Souls*, pp. 24–25.

8. Du Bois, "The Superior Race," *Smart Set* 70, no. 4 (April 1923): 60 (hereafter "Superior Race"); and see *Dusk of Dawn* (New York: Oxford University Press, 2007; originally published in 1940), p. 77 (hereafter *Dusk of Dawn*).

9. *Souls*, p. 1.

10. W. E. B. Du Bois, *Worlds of Color* (New York: Oxford University Press, 2007; originally published in 1961), p. 240.

11. We find Du Bois here in a rare moment of modesty. W. E. B. Du Bois, "The Souls of Black Folk," *The Independent* 57, no. 2920 (November 17, 1904): 1152, http://www .webdubois.org/dbSouls-1904Essay.html, accessed July 10, 2013. *Souls* had many distinguished admirers. William James dispatched a copy to his brother Henry on June 6, 1903, very soon after it first appeared. "I am sending you a decidedly moving book by a mulatto ex-student of mine, Dubois, professor [of] history at Atlanta (Georgia) negro College. Read Chapters VII to XI for local color, etc." William James and Henry James, *William and Henry James Selected Letters*, ed. Ignas K. Skrupskelis and Elizabeth M. Berkeley (Charlottesville: University of Virginia Press, 1997), p. 431. Henry James commended *Souls,* somewhat backhandedly, in *The American Scene* (1907), as "the only 'Southern' book of any distinction published in many a year" in the course of a complaint about what he called the "vacancy" of Southern culture. With slavery

gone, James thought, it was as if there was nothing else left to reflect upon. "Had the *only* focus of life then been Slavery? . . . To say 'yes' seems the only way to account for the degree of the vacancy, and yet even as I form that word I meet as a reproach the face of the beautiful old house I just mentioned, whose ample spaces had so unmistakably echoed to the higher amenities that one seemed to feel the accumulated traces and tokens gradually come out of their corners like blest objects taken one by one from a reliquary worn with much handling." Henry James, *The American Scene* (New York: Harper and Brothers, 1907), p. 402.

12. W. E. B. Du Bois, *Black Reconstruction in America: An Essay toward History of the Part Which Black Folk Played in the Attempt to Reconstruct Democracy in America, 1860–1880* (New York: Oxford University Press, 2007; originally published in 1935), p. 580.

13. See August Meier's classic study *Negro Thought in America: 1880–1915* (Ann Arbor: University of Michigan Press, 1964), pp. 19–25; and C. Vann Woodward, *Reunion and Reaction: The Compromise of 1877 and the End of Reconstruction* (New York: Oxford University Press, 1991), pp. 214–215; for emigrationism, see David Brion Davis "Exiles, Exodus and Promised Lands" (The Tanner Lecture on Human Values, Stanford University, Stanford, CA, February 22–23, 2006), http://tannerlectures.utah.edu/_documents/a-to-z/d/Davis_2007.pdf, accessed July 10, 2013.

14. *Dusk of Dawn,* p. 16.

15. See W. E. B. Du Bois, *The Correspondence of W. E. B. Du Bois,* vol. 1: *Selections, 1877–1934,* ed. Herbert Aptheker (Amherst: University of Massachusetts Press, 1973), p. 17 (hereafter *Correspondence*).

16. *Autobiography,* p. 96.
17. Hamilton Beck, "W. E. B. Du Bois as a Study Abroad Student in Germany, 1892–1894," *Frontiers: The Interdisciplinary Journal of Study Abroad* 2, no. 1 (Fall 1996): 45–63, http://www.frontiersjournal.com/issues/vol2/vol2-03 _Beck.htm, accessed July 10, 2013 (hereafter "Study Abroad Student").
18. *Correspondence,* 1:28.
19. Recounted in *Darkwater,* p. 8—an earlier version of the essay appeared in *The Crisis* 15, no. 4 (February 1918): 167–171—and *Autobiography,* p. 115. Du Bois frequently spoke of his Lehrjahre, his Wanderjahre, and his Meisterjahre, perhaps echoing the titles of Goethe's *Wilhelm Meisters Lehrjahre* [Wilhelm Meister's apprenticeship] (1795–1796)—often said to be the first Bildungsroman—his *Wilhelm Meisters Wanderjahre* (1821) [Wilhelm Meister's journeyman years] and Johannes Pustkuchen's parodic *Wilhelm Meisters Meisterjahre* (1824) [Wilhelm Meister's master years], whose titles mark the traditional stages—from apprentice to journeyman to master—in the medieval European craft guild.
20. W. E. B. Du Bois, *The Suppression of the African Slave Trade* (New York: Oxford University Press, 2007; originally published in 1896), p. xxxi.
21. *Darkwater,* p. 9.
22. "Evolving Program," p. 60.
23. Eulogizing Stalin, in 1953, Du Bois wrote, "His judgment of men was profound." Du Bois's was erratic. "He early saw through the flamboyance and exhibitionism of Trotsky, who fooled the world, and especially America," Du Bois went on. "The whole ill-bred and insulting attitude of Liberals in the U.S. today began with our naive

acceptance of Trotsky's magnificent lying propaganda, which he carried around the world. Against it, Stalin stood like a rock and moved neither right nor left, as he continued to advance toward a real socialism instead of the sham Trotsky offered." Du Bois, "On Stalin," *National Guardian,* March 16, 1953, reprinted in W. E. B. Du Bois, *Newspaper Columns by Du Bois,* ed. Herbert Aptheker (White Plains, NY: Kraus-Thomson, 1986), vol. 2, p. 910. Du Bois emerged from his seventies a rather doctrinaire Communist, refusing even to criticize the Soviet invasion of Hungary in 1956. David Levering Lewis notes that Du Bois had fervid praise for Mao at a time when tens of millions of Chinese were dying of starvation: "As they moved about Beijing in their ceremonial cocoon, Du Bois and [his wife] Graham Du Bois knew absolutely nothing of the catastrophe inflicted upon the Chinese people by their omnipotent ruler." David Levering Lewis, *W. E. B. Du Bois, 1919–1963: The Fight for Equality and the American Century* (New York: Henry Holt, 2000), p. 563 (hereafter *W. E. B. Du Bois, 1919–1963*).

24. Gerald Horne, *Black and Red: W. E. B. Du Bois and the Afro-American Response to the Cold War* (Albany, NY: SUNY Press, 1985), p. 337.

25. W. E. B. Du Bois, "The Talented Tenth," in Booker T. Washington et al., *The Negro Problem* (New York: James Pott & Co., 1903), p. 33.

26. *Dusk of Dawn,* p. 74. The passage continues: "Such is the soul of the Negro."

27. "Criteria of Negro Art," *The Crisis* (1926), in *Writings,* ed. Nathan Irving Huggins (New York: Library of America, 1986), p. 1000 (hereafter *Writings*).

28. David Levering Lewis, *W. E. B. Du Bois, 1868–1919: Biography of a Race* (New York: Henry Holt, 1993), p. 10 (hereafter *Biography of a Race*); and see Edward J. Blum, *W. E. B. Du Bois: American Prophet* (Philadelphia: University of Pennsylvania Press, 2007), p. 213.

29. *Autobiography,* p. 106.

30. *National Guardian,* May 31, 1954, cited in Lewis, *W. E. B. Du Bois, 1919–1963,* p. 557.

CHAPTER ONE: THE AWAKENING

1. Lewis, *Biography of a Race,* pp. 128–129.

2. *Autobiography,* p. 102. The saying derives from lines of the poet Josef Viktor von Scheffel: "Behüet dich Gott! es wär zu schön gewesen,/Behüet dich Gott, es hat nicht sollen sein!" (Godspeed! It would have too been lovely,/Godspeed, it was not to be!" Josef Viktor von Scheffel, *Der Trompeter von Säkkingen: Ein sang vom Oberrhein* (Boston: Ginn and Company, 1906), p. 227.

3. His courses are listed in letters Du Bois sent to the Slater Fund (*Correspondence,* pp. 21–28).

   There are additional details in the exact list of Du Bois's completed courses, which Ingeborg H. Solbrig has retrieved from the university archives. See her "American Slavery in Eighteenth-Century German Literature: The Case of Herder's 'Neger-Idyllen,' " *Monatshefte* 82, no. 1 (Spring 1990): 38–49 (hereafter "Herder's 'Neger-Idyllen' "). A well-researched account of Du Bois's Berlin days appears in Hamilton Beck, "Study Abroad Student," pp. 45–63. See also Lewis, *Biography of a Race,* pp. 127–131; *Autobiography,* pp. 99–102; and Francis L. Broderick,

"German Influence on the Scholarship of W. E. B. Du Bois," *Phylon* 19, no. 4 (1958): 367–371 (hereafter "German Influence").

4. This is from an account he wrote at the time in his journals, reproduced in the *Autobiography,* p. 106.

5. *Darkwater,* p. 9.

6. Cited in Kenneth Barkin, "W. E. B. Du Bois' Love Affair with Imperial Germany," *German Studies Review* 28, no. 2 (May 2005): 289, quoting *The Reminiscences of W. E. B. Du Bois,* ed. William Ingersoll (New York: Columbia University Oral History Research Office, 1963), pp. 114–115.

7. *Darkwater,* p. 8.

8. *Autobiography,* p. 99. And see Barkin, "Du Bois' Love Affair," 294; especially his suggestive reading of one of Du Bois's "The Winds of Time" columns from *The Chicago Defender,* January 7, 1948. In an essay from 1894, Du Bois wrote of the railway-carriage experience of being mistaken for a gentleman from English-speaking India. "The Afro-American," *Journal of Transnational American Studies* 2, no. 1 (2010), http://escholarship.ucop.edu/uc/item/2pm9g4q2, accessed July 10, 2013.

9. *Darkwater,* p. 8.

10. The Christian-Social Party (Christlich-soziale Partei, CSP) was created to combine progressive views on labor questions—social insurance, an eight-hour working day, progressive income taxes—with conservative Christian moral views and monarchism; and so to combat the more revolutionary Social Democratic party. Its founder was the Kaiser's domestic chaplain.

11. *Autobiography,* p. 103.

12. Rudolf von Gneist, *History of the English Parliament* (London: William Clowes and Sons, 1889; translated by

A. H. Keane), p. xiv. For Lenz, see Michael Oakeshott, "The Historiography of Max Lenz," in *What Is History? and Other Essays* (Exeter: Imprint Academic, 2004), pp. 342–343; August Meitzen, *Die Mitverantwortlichkeit der Gebildeten und Besitzenden für das Wohl der arbeitenden Klassen: Zur socialen und religiösen Bewegung* (Berlin: W. Hertz, 1876).

13. *Autobiography,* p. 166.

14. The Kathedersozialisten were radical only by somewhat conservative standards. Schmoller was a monarchist. He believed that the Kaiser (and the civil service) should play a neutral independent role in mediating the conflicts between the working classes and the propertied classes. Gustav Schmoller, "Die soziale Frage und der Preußische Staat" (The Social Question and the Prussian State), *Preußischer Jahrbücher* 33 (1874): 323–342 (hereafter "The Social Question"). But he did have a real (if occasionally condescending) sympathy for the sufferings of the working classes: "ist der einzelne Arbeiter daran schuld, daß er vielfach in Höhlen wohnt, die ihn zum Tier oder zum Verbrecher degradieren? . . . ist er daran schuld, daß seine arbeitsteilige, mechanische Beschäftigung ihn weniger lernen läßt, als früher Lehrling und Geselle in der Werkstatt lernte?" ("Is the individual worker at fault, because he often lives in dens that degrade him to the level of an animal or a criminal? . . . Is he at fault, because his specialized, mechanical, employment permits him to learn less than apprentices and journeymen learned in their workshops?") Cited in Hans Michael Heinig, *Der Sozialstaat im Dienst der Freiheit* (Tübingen: Mohr Siebeck, 2008), p. 95.

15. Du Bois's notebook is quoted in Broderick, "German Influence," 369; and see Lemke, "Berlin," 53. Reginald

Hansen, "Schmoller as a Scientist of Political Economy," in Jurgen Georg Backhaus, ed., *Handbook of the History of Economic Thought* (New York: Springer, 2012), p. 400. A notably lucid and elegant account of the historical school can be found in Bruce Caldwell, *Hayek's Challenge* (Chicago: University of Chicago Press, 2005), pp. 39–82.

16. Nicholas Balabkins, *Not by Theory Alone . . . : The Economics of Gustav von Schmoller and Its Legacy to America* (Berlin: Duncker & Humblot, 1988), p. 41.

17. Cited in Albion Small, "Some Contributions to the History of Sociology. Section XV. The Restoration of Ethics in Economic Theory. The Professorial Socialists. The Verein für Socialpolitik," *American Journal of Sociology* 29, no. 6 (May 1924): 709, 710. Wagner's audience was the annual conference of the Evangelical Church of Prussia, which was a pretty conservative group. Writing in 1924, Small observed, "If the head of the department of economics at Princeton should pronounce the same judgment today, in terms of bolshevists and bolshevism, in a session of the Presbyterian General Assembly, it would be less sensational than Wagner's utterance in its time and place," p. 709.

18. See Axel Schäfer's important article "W. E. B. Du Bois, German Social Thought, and the Racial Divide in American Progressivism, 1892–1909," in *The Journal of American History* 88, no. 3 (2001): 925–949 and especially 938 (hereafter "German Social Thought"); and S. P. Altman, "Schmoller's Political Economy," *Journal of Political Economy* 13, no. 1 (December 1904): 83.

19. "Das Rechtsgefühl der Masse vertheidigt jede bestehende Eigentumsordnung, die derselben auch nur ganz ungefähr mit den Tugenden, den Kenntnissen und Leistun-

gen der Einzelnen wie der verschiedenen Klassen im Einklang zu sein scheint. Umgekehrt aber ist jede Besitz- und Einkommensordnung . . . mit der Zeit gefallen, wenn sie nicht mehr auf diese Ueberzeugung sich stützen konnte. Der Nagel zum Sarg jeder bestehenden Eigenthumsvertheilung ist der um sich greifende Glaube, daß moralisch verwerfliche Erwerbsarten zu ungehindert sich breit machen, daß mehr der unehrliche als der ehrliche Erwerb die großen Vermögen schaffe, daß zwischen den verschiedenen Leistungen der Einzelnen und ihren wirtschaftlichen Resultaten—ihrem Einkommen eine zu große, zu ungerechte Disharmonie sei." (The sense of justice of the masses vindicates any existing system of property that seems, even if only roughly, in accord with the virtues, knowledge and accomplishments of the individual as of the different classes. Conversely, however, every system of property and income . . . has collapsed over time if it can no longer support this conviction. The nail in the coffin of any existing system of property is when the belief takes hold that morally reprehensible forms of trade are spreading without hindrance, that dishonorable rather than honorable trades are making great fortunes, that there is too great, too unjust, a discrepancy between the different accomplishments of individuals and their economic results—that is their incomes.) Schmoller, "The Social Question," 334. Note how the argument for reform is underwritten by historical generalizations: It is the repeated collapse of systems of property that have lost their moral legitimacy in the past that suggests that we face the same risk today.

20. "Die griechischen Staatsideale, das römische Amtsrecht in der Zeit des Freistaates, das harte Imperium der

Cäsaren, das durch das Christentum humanisierte Recht des Mittelalters, die mittelalterliche Kirche mit ihren Institutionen, die aufkommende moderne Staatsgewalt, der aufgeklärte Despotismus mit seinen Kämpfen gegen das feudal-ständische Klassenregiment, mit seiner Bemühung um ein gutes Gerichtswesen, um eine lautere Verwaltung, die neueren konstitutionelle Verfassungen mit ihren Rechtsgarantien, die Versuche der neuen Demokratie den unteren Klassen eine bessere und gerechtere Stellung zu verschaffen, das sind alles Stationen auf dem schwierigen, dornenvollen Wege der Menschheit, zu einer großen und festen Regierung ohne zu viel Klassenmißbräuche zu kommen." (Greek ideals of government, Roman law in the period of the republic, the harsh rule of the Caesars, law in the middle ages, humanized by Christianity, the church in the middle ages and its institutions, enlightened despotism with its struggles against the feudal rank-based class rule and its efforts for a good judiciary and a fairer administration, the new constitutions with their guarantees of rights, the attempts of the new democracies to obtain a better and more just place for the lower classes: these are all steps on the difficult, thorny path of mankind to a greater, more stable regime without too much class abuse.) Gustav Schmoller, *Die Soziale Frage: Klassenbildung, Arbeiterfrage, Klassenkampf* (Munich: von Duncker & Humblot, 1918), pp. 627–628 (hereafter *Soziale Frage: Klassenbildung*).

21. "Alle Klassenkämpfe erscheinen als die Folge dessen, was man Klassenherrschaft nennt. . . . Man versteht . . . unter Klassenherrschaft . . . die Abhängigkeit der schwachen von der starken Klasse, die dadurch entsteht, daß die

letzter Staatsgewalt beeinflußt und beherrscht, daß sie nicht bloß wirtschaftliche Überlegenheit, sondern die politische Macht, die Staatshoheitrechte, die Amtsgewalt für ihre Sonderzwecke, für ihren wirtschaftlichen Vorteil ausnutzt." (All class struggle appears as the consequence of what we call class domination. . . . One understands . . . by class domination . . . the dependence of the weaker on the stronger class, which is a result of the fact that the latter influence and rule the exercise of state power, and that they use political power, state sovereignty and authority for their own particular purposes.) Schmoller, *Soziale Frage: Klassenbildung,* pp. 624–625.

22. "Wo es verschiedene Klassen gibt, haben sie einerseits verschiedene, getrennte, ja entgegengesetzte Interessen, andererseits aber auch gemeinsame; die ersteren sind überwiegend äußerer, praktischer und wirtschaftlicher Art, sind auf die nächsten Ziele gerichtet, die letzteren sind mehr ideeller und geistiger Art, sind auf die Gesamtzwecke der Gesellschaft, des Staates und die Zukunft gerichtet." (Where there are different classes, they have, on the one hand, different, separate, even conflicting interests, but, on the other hand, also interests in common; the former are predominantly of an external, practical, economic nature, and are directed towards near-term goals; the latter are more idealistic and spiritual in nature, and are directed towards the overall purposes of the society, the state and the future.) Schmoller, *Soziale Frage: Klassenbildung,* p. 620.

23. W. E. B. Du Bois, *The Philadelphia Negro* (New York: Oxford University Press, 2007; originally published in 1899), p. 2 (hereafter *Philadelphia Negro*).

24. *Philadelphia Negro,* pp. 269–270.

25. One of Marx's early works, *Zur Judenfrage* (On the Jewish question) (1844), was a response to an essay by Bruno Bauer, another of the young Hegelians, on the same topic. The focus of these discussions is on Jews as a religious group—Bauer argues that Jewish emancipation (i.e., the granting of full civil rights) requires Jews to abandon their religion—but he also does say (in a later essay) that the Jewish question "is to be understood as a national question, concerning the mutual compatibility of different forms of Sittlichkeit" (Dennis Moggach, *The Philosophy and Politics of Bruno Bauer* [Cambridge, MA: Cambridge University Press, 2007], p. 140). So both the idea that the question of the civil rights of a group, X, should be called the "X-frage," and the idea that these could be seen as like national questions were natural enough. Du Bois, responding to a commission from Max Weber, later published a paper titled "Die Negerfrage in den Vereinigten Staaten" in Weber's *Archiv für Sozialwissenschaft und Sozialpolitik* 22 (January 1906): 31–79. (This paper clearly reflects the work he had done for the Berlin dissertation he was never able to submit.) Robert Gooding-Williams, noting the congruences between Schmoller's work on the Social Question and Du Bois's on the Negro Problem, views Du Bois as hobbled by his shared conception of the poor as "an uncultivated mass." He contrasts Du Bois's analysis with another picture of the Negro Problem, which he finds adumbrated in Frederick Douglass's *My Bondage and My Freedom.* On the latter picture, the Negro's problem is not black exclusion but white supremacy. The young Du Bois saw the social exclusion of black people as an anomaly, a betrayal of the basic ideals

of the American republic; Douglass regarded the oppression of black people as a "central and defining feature of" the "institutional fabric of American life." And oppression is not about exclusion but about domination. It means keeping blacks not out but down. The solution then can't be mere integration, the end of exclusion; rather, it requires the re-imagination of American citizenship as a citizenship of racial equals. It means the end of subordination. See Robert Gooding-Williams, *In the Shadow of Du Bois: Afro-Modern Political Thought in America* (Cambridge, MA: Harvard University Press, 2009), pp. 56, 15.

26. "Und wir werden so sagen können, von den ältesten Zeiten bis auf den heutigen Tag sei jeder erhebliche Rassengegensatz mit seinen materiellen und psychischen Folgen ein wichtiges Element der Klassengegensätze für die Staaten, in denen er vorhanden ist." (And we can say that, from the earliest times to the present day, every substantial racial conflict with its material and psychological consequences is an important element of class conflict, for the states in which it exists.) Schmoller, *Soziale Frage: Klassenbildung*, pp. 519–520.

27. Barkin, "Du Bois' Love Affair," 299–300 (citing the Berlin Sketches, Du Bois Papers, Reel 87, frame 482). Du Bois's student assessment of the two was shrewd. Wagner's "hobby is the discovery of the golden mean between the warring extremes of his science," he wrote. "He comes dangerously near committing the common mistake in such cases of mistaking his extremes. He is publishing a new edition of his valuable *Lehrbuch,* and as inducement is offering various blandishments to the national apparition of socialism. The *bête noire* of the

German economist is, of course, the British school founded, as Wagner says, with a jerk of his head, by 'Adahm Smiss.' Wagner, however, gives them due credit for their great work and agrees with them more fully than with the younger German radicals headed by Schmoller." And, he noted correctly, "There is evidently no intellectual love lost between Wagner and Schmoller." *Autobiography*, p. 166.

28. W. E. B. Du Bois, *The Correspondence of W. E. B. Du Bois,* vol. 1: *Selections, 1877–1934,* ed. Herbert Aptheker (Amherst: University of Massachusetts Press, 1973), p. 25.

29. Axel Schäfer, "German Social Thought," 934.

30. Quoted in Erik Grimmer-Solem, *The Rise of Historical Economics and Social Reform in Germany, 1864–1894* (New York: Oxford University Press, 2003), p. 179.

31. Schmoller, cited in Rudolf Richter, "Bridging Old and New Institutional Economics: Gustav Schmoller, the Leader of the Younger German Historical School, Seen with Neo-institutionalists' Eyes," *Journal of Institutional and Theoretical Economics* 152, no. 4 (December 1996): 575, 574 (hereafter "Bridging Old and New"). For the concept of *Volkswirtschaft* see Israel M. Kirzner, "Economics, the Economy, and the "Volkswirtschaft,'" in Laurence S. Moss, ed., *The Economic Point of View: An Essay in the History of Economic Thought* (Kansas City: Sheed Andrews McMeel, 1976), http://oll.libertyfund.org/title/304/5936, accessed July 10, 2013.

32. Today's general economics "is of a philosophical-sociological character" and is "based on the nature of society and the general causes of economic life and behavior . . . its typical organizations and their developments, its most important institutions statically and dy-

namically." Cited in Richter, "Bridging Old and New," 574–575.

33. For that matter, Wagner's political anti-Semitism grew so vehement that it cost him the support of the Conservative caucus in 1885, and his seat in Parliament. See Evalyn A. Clark, "Adolf Wagner: From National Economist to National Socialist," *Political Science Quarterly* 55, no. 3 (September 1940): 378–411; the quote is on p. 386.

34. Andrew Zimmerman, *Alabama in Africa: Booker T. Washington, the German Empire, and the Globalization of the New South* (Princeton: Princeton University Press, 2010), p. 105 (hereafter *Alabama*).

35. Dr. Rudolph Virchow, "Anthropology in the Last Twenty Years," in Rudolph Virchow, M. Ingwald Unset, and Paul Topinard, *Anthropological Papers* (Washington, DC: Government Printing Office, 1891), p. 563. (This was Virchow's opening address to the twentieth general meeting of the German Anthropological Association in Vienna, August 5, 1889.)

36. *Autobiography*, p. 104. As it happens, Schmoller himself seems to have had old-fashioned views about Negroes: "They eat human flesh and kill from passion without a sting of conscience; they could die from homesickness, but every tune makes them dance." (Quoted in Zimmerman, *Alabama*, p. 110.) Even Virchow could not entirely escape the racialism of his era. In *Anthropology and Antihumanism in Imperial Germany*, Andrew Zimmerman describes a large survey that Rudolf Virchow undertook in which he carefully compared the racial characteristics of Jews and Germans and (with no prejudicial intent) established to his satisfaction that the Jews had a separate national origin and came from distinct racial stock.

(Andrew Zimmerman, *Anthropology and Antihumanism in Imperial Germany* [Chicago: University of Chicago Press, 2001], p. 137.) The younger Du Bois, as has often been noted, was not innocent of the commonplace anti-Semitism of his time and place. In an essay on "The Present Condition of German Politics" in 1893, he wrote, "It may surprise one at first to see a recrudescence of anti-Jewish feeling in a civilized state at this late day. One must learn however that the basis of the neo-antisemitism is economic and its end socialism. Only its present motive force is racial hatred. It must be ever remembered that the great capitalists of Germany, the great leaders of industry are Jews; moreover, banded together by oppression in the past, they work for each other, and aided by the vast power of their wealth, and their great natural abilities, they have forced citadel after citadel, until now they practically control the stock-market, own the press, fill the bar and bench, are crowding the professions—indeed there seems to be no limit to the increase of their power. This of course is a menace to the newly nationalized country." Du Bois, "The Present Condition of German Politics," *Central European History* 31, no. 3 (1998): 170–187. (The essay was written in 1893, when its sentiments would have been controversial, alas, almost nowhere.) The original version of *Souls* has a handful of invidious references to Jews and their sharp dealings. (In a revision, decades later, he changed these references to "immigrants." (See George Bornstein, "W. E. B. Du Bois and the Jews: Ethics, Editing, and *The Souls of Black Folk*," *Textual Cultures* 1, no. 1 [Spring 2006]: 64–74.) But for most of his adult life, Du Bois was concertedly *anti*-anti-Semitic. After he visited Nazi Germany for six months in

1936—taking in a performance of "Lohengrin" at Bayreuth—he wrote frankly (in the Pittsburgh *Courier*) that the "campaign of race prejudice . . . surpasses in vindictive cruelty and public insult anything I have ever seen; and I have seen much." And he went on: "There has been no tragedy in modern times equal in its awful effects to the fight on the Jew in Germany. It is an attack on civilization comparable only to such horrors as the Spanish Inquisition and the African Slave trade." (Cited in Lewis, *W. E. B. Du Bois, 1919–1963*, p. 400.) These words were written, remember, before the campaign of mass-murder began.

37. *Autobiography*, p. 104; again quoting from notes he made at the time. Arnold Rampersad astutely notes, "It was perfectly consistent with Du Bois's thought that he should be fascinated by this romantic authoritarianism or incipient fascism." Arnold Rampersad, *The Art and Imagination of W. E. B. Du Bois* (Cambridge, MA: Harvard University Press, 1976), p. 45 (hereafter *Art and Imagination*).

38. *Philadelphia Negro*, p. 225.

39. "What occasionally oppresses a genius by appearing to be a narrowing fetter is for the inert majority a wholesome spur to activity and progress," Treitschke went on. "The generations of a people's life are joined together and limited by a community of views about life, from which even the strong man can not break away." (Cited in Albion Woodbury Small, *Origins of Sociology* [New York: Russell and Russell, 1924], pp. 277–278.) Treitschke had his own argument against the sort of reforms favored by the Verein: It would mess with the Absolute represented by the Teutonic social order. He also warned that the sort of social-welfare measures that Schmoller favored

would promote socialist revolution, rather than prevent it, and advised that "no social reform could offer the working class a greater blessing than the old simple appeal: pray and work!" Quoted in Andreas Dorpalen, *Heinrich von Treitschke* (Port Washington, NY: Kennikat Press, 1973), p. 200.

CHAPTER TWO: CULTURE AND COSMOPOLITANISM

1. For a Herder-focused discussion of Du Bois's Berlin days, see Solbrig, "Herder's 'Neger-Idyllen.'"

2. Raymond Williams, *Keywords: A Vocabulary of Culture and Society* (New York: Oxford University Press, 1985), p. 89. Herder and his circle used a number of related words, including *Geist des Volkes* and *Seele des Volkes* and *Nationalgeist;* scholars have suggested that the specific term *Volksgeist* may have been introduced by Georg Friedrich Puchta or Joachim Heinrich Campe. Friedrich von Savigny did much to popularize it. Apparently Herder can get credit for introducing the term "nationalism" (or, anyway, *Nationalismus*).

3. "Das Menschengeschlecht ist ein Ganzes: wir arbeiten und dulden, säen und ernten für einander." Johann Gottfried Herder, *Briefe zur Beförderung der Humanität,* in *J. G. Herder: Werke,* vol. 7 (Frankfurt am Main: Deutscher Klassiker Verlag, 1991), p. 735. And the title of chapter 1 of book 7 of the *Ideen sur Philsophie der Geschichte der Menschheit* (1784) is "In so verschiednen Formen das Menschengeschlecht auf der Erde erscheint: so ists doch überall ein' und dieselbe Menschengattung." (In however many varieties humankind appears on the earth, it's still everywhere one and the same human species.) That's

not to say, of course, that he was a thoroughgoing racial egalitarian in the contemporary manner.

4. *Souls,* p. 543. Writing in 1924, Du Bois made the comparison with romantic nationalism explicit: "Exactly the same thing was happening in Negro America that happened in Germany when she discovered resources within her own soul that made her independent of French culture." Du Bois, "The Dilemma of the Negro," *American Mercury* 3 (October 1924): 180.

5. *Souls,* p. 52.

6. *Souls,* p. 114. (Thanks to Alex Ross, I have seen a copy of Du Bois's ticket to the performance of *Lohengrin* in Bayreuth on Wednesday, August 19, 1936, at 4:00 p.m. As we saw, he continued to care for this particular opera.)

7. In the previous poem, "Die rechte Hand," Herder calls the white master "der weiße Teufel." Johann Gottfried von Herder, *Briefe zu Beförderung der Humanität,* Zehnte Sammlung (1797), Brief 114. "Neger-Idyllen." See Solbrig, "Herder's 'Neger-Idyllen.'"

8. Herder, "On the Change of Taste," in Johann Gottfried Herder, *Philosophical Writings,* ed. Michael N. Foster (Cambridge: Cambridge University Press, 2002), p. 256 (hereafter "Change of Taste"); discussed by Sonia Sikka, *Herder on Humanity and Cultural Difference: Enlightened Relativism* (Cambridge: Cambridge University Press, 2011), p. 27.; cf. Charles Taylor, "The Importance of Herder," in *Philosophical Arguments* (Cambridge, MA: Harvard University Press, 1995), pp. 83–87.

9. Herder, "Change of Taste," p. 255.

10. Johann Gottfried Herder, *Outlines of a Philosophy of the History of Man,* trans. T. Churchill (New York: Bergman

Publishers, 1966), p. 146. Hereafter *Outlines*. This is a facsimile of the 1800 London edition.

11. In the same chapter, Herder laments the scarcity of reliable information about the societies of Africa: "But how many happy and peaceful nations may dwell at the feet of the Mountains of the Moon! Europeans are unworthy to behold their happiness; for they have unpardonably sinned, and still continue to sin, against this quarter of the Globe." Herder, "Outlines," p. 149. In 1785, Kant skeptically reviewed Herder's *Ideas for the Philosophy of the History of Humanity* (the first two of its three volumes, anyway) raising an eyebrow, in particular, at its moments of racial fraternity; and yet, as Sander Gilman notes, Kant, in subsequent excursions into physical anthropology, never resumed his earlier derogation toward the African, maintaining, instead, a resolute pose of neutrality. Sander L. Gilman, "The Figure of the Black in German Aesthetic Theory," *Eighteenth-Century Studies* 8, no. 4 (Summer 1975): 387–389.

12. See Hans Adler, "Herder's Concept of Humanität," in Hans Adler and Wulf Kopke et al., *A Companion to the Works of Johann Gottfried Herder* (Rochester, NY: Camden House, 2009), p. 97.

13. Friedrich Meinecke, *Cosmopolitanism and the National State,* trans. Robert B. Kimber (Princeton: Princeton University Press, 1970), p. 94. Originally published in 1908 as *Weltbürgertum und Nationalstaat: Studien zur Genesis des deutschen Nationalstaats.* Meinecke is discussing Fichte at this point; but he has expressed the same claim in various ways by this point in discussions of Humboldt, Novalis, and Schlegel.

14. Giuseppe Mazzini, *An Essay On the Duties of Man Addressed to Workingmen* (New York: Funk & Wagnalls, 1898), pp. 57–58; Edmund Burke, *Reflections on the Revolution in France,* ed. J. C. D. Clark (Stanford: Stanford University Press, 2001), p. 202.

15. "The Conservation of Races," in W. E. B. Du Bois, *The Oxford W. E. B. Du Bois Reader,* ed. Eric J. Sundquist (New York: Oxford University Press, 1996), p. 40 (hereafter "Conservation").

16. "O Deutschland, wann werden deine eigenen Söhne aufhören, dich mit ihrer fanatischen Objektivität zum Tode verwunden. Wann wird endlich ein gesunder nationaler Egoismus bei aller Schonung der Rechte Andrer zuerst an das Wohl des eigenen Staats denken und dem unglückseligen Kosmopolitismus weichen, mit dem wir jede berechtigte und unberechtigte Empfindlichkeit des Auslands schonen!" Adolf Wagner, *Elsass und Lothringen und ihre Wiedergewinnung für Deutschland* (Alsace and Lorraine and Winning them back for Germany), 3rd ed. (Leipzig: Duncker and Humblot, 1870), p. 87. In an autobiography published after the First World War, Meinecke remarked that in *Cosmopolitanism and the National State* he had represented the "liberation of purely national thinking and action from universalistic, cosmopolitan motives" as "a great achievement of the middle-nineteenth century." ("hatte ich in '*Weltbürgertum und Nationalstaat*' die Befreiung des rein staatlichen Denkens und Handelns von universalistischen, weltbürgerlichen Motiven als eine große Errungenschaft des mittleren 19 Jahrhunderts dargestellt.") Friedrich Meinecke, *Erlebtes, 1862–1919* (Stuttgart: Köhler, 1964), p. 286; cited in Mark W. Clark, *Beyond*

Catastrophe: German Intellectuals and Cultural Renewal after World War II, 1945–1955 (Oxford: Lexington Books, 2006), p. 18. The nationalists picked the fight with the cosmopolitans. It should be noted that cosmopolitan *anti*-nationalism doesn't really emerge until the 1920s.

17. "I am never alone./Many who lived before me/And strove at a distance from me,/Wove,/Wove/My being." "Wenn die Uhren so nah" (When the clocks so close) (1898) in Rainer Maria Rilke, *Die Gedichte* (Leipzig: Insel Verlag, 1996), p. 194.

18. A. O. Lovejoy argued that the idea predated Goethe . . . but he, too, insisted on the pervasiveness of the theme. A. O. Lovejoy, *The Great Chain of Being* (Cambridge, MA: Harvard University Press, 1964), p. 250.

19. *Souls,* p. 3. Note the evident echo here of the Faust passage in the epigraph to this chapter. There have been many fine scholarly discussions of the American sources of Du Bois's idea of double consciousness, including Dickson D. Bruce Jr., "W. E. B. Du Bois and the Idea of Double Consciousness," *American Literature* 64, no. 2 (June 1992): 299–309; Werner Sollers, *Beyond Ethnicity: Consent and Descent in American Culture* (New York: Oxford University Press, 1986), pp. 232, 247–253; Eric Sundquist, *To Wake the Nations: Race in the Making of American Literature* (Cambridge, MA: Harvard University Press, 1998), pp. 570–573; Rampersad, *Art and Imagination*, p. 74; and Shamoon Zamir, *Dark Voices* (Chicago: University of Chicago Press, 1995), pp. 99, 116–117. As Zamir observes, references to "double consciousness" were common in late nineteenth-century experimental psychology. Eugène Azam's *Hypnotisme, double conscience, et altérations de la personnalité* (Paris: Librairie J.-B Baillière et

Fils, 1887) is a study of what came to be called multiple (or dissociative) personality disorder. In 1889, Alfred Binet, the great French experimental psychologist, who corresponded with James, published a book, *On Double Consciousness: Experimental Psychological Studies* (Chicago: Open Court Publishing Co., 1896), 2nd ed., that discusses Azam's work and reports his own explorations of the way in which "hysterical" or hypnotized patients, who reported no sensation in a hand, could nevertheless display intelligent behavior with that hand, of which they were unaware. (We should now probably think of this in terms of split consciousness—the extreme version of which occurs in some people who have undergone brain bisection. See R. W. Sperry, "Hemisphere Deconnection and Unity in Conscious Awareness," *American Psychologist* 23, no. 10 [October 1968]: 723–733.) As I say, James was aware of the work of Azam and Binet (who are important figures in the history of theories of hypnotism). See also Dan Zahavi, "Unity of Consciousness and the Problem of the Self," in Shaun Gallagher, ed., *The Oxford Handbook of the Self* (Oxford: Oxford University Press, 2011), p. 317. Ian Hacking identifies a distinct history of use of the term, going back at least to 1817, in his "Double Consciousness in Britain: 1815–1975," *Dissociation* 4, no. 3 (September 1991): 134–146. But all these uses of the idea of double consciousness, rooted in psychopathology, seem a poor model for what Du Bois had in mind. All they share with Du Bois is the idea that a single body might be literally or metaphorically inhabited by two consciousnesses, aware of each other or not.

20. *Souls,* p. 3. This formulation first appears in print in August 1897, in "Strivings of the Negro People" in the

Atlantic Monthly and is expressed more emphatically here in *Souls*. There are frequent references to the message of the Negro in "The Conservation of Races," given as a talk to the new American Negro Academy in 1897, which I discuss below.

21. G. W. F. Hegel, *Phänomenologie des Geistes* (Munich: GRIN Verlag, 2009), p. 162.

22. Du Bois implicitly suggests one's sense of an ethnic identity is determined by its boundaries, as much as its internal content, much as Fredrik Barth would argue in 1969; Fredrik Barth, "Introduction," in *Ethnic Groups and Boundaries: The Social Organization of Culture Difference* (Long Grove, IL: Waveland Press, 1998), pp. 9–57. George Palmer speaks of Hegel's notion that the knowledge of a limit is a knowledge beyond that limit. He imagines encountering Kasper Hauser, locked in his little room. Hauser says he has been there ever since he was born. What does he know? Nothing, Hauser complains, beyond the walls of this room. Palmer: "Might I not fairly reply, 'You contradict yourself. How can you know anything of the walls of a room unless you know of much beyond them?' We cannot conceive of a limit except as a limit from something." George Herbert Palmer, *The Nature of Goodness* (Boston: Houghton Mifflin, 1903), p. 139 (hereafter *Nature of Goodness*).

23. W. E. B. Du Bois, "To the Nations of the World," in Philip Sheldon Foner and Robert James Branham, eds., *Lift Every Voice: African American Oratory, 1787–1900* (Tuscaloosa: University of Alabama Press, 1998), pp. 906–907.

24. *Souls,* p. 8.

25. "Durch Verbindungen also, die aus dem Innern der Wesen entspringen, muss einer den Reichtum des anderen

sich eigen machen. Eine solche charakter-bildende Verbindung ist, nach der Erfahrung aller auch sogar der rohesten Nationen, z.B. die Verbindung der beiden Geschlechter. . . . Der bildende Nutzen solcher Verbindungen beruht immer auf dem Grade, in welchem sich die Selbständigkeit der Verbundenen zugleich mit der Innigkeit der Verbindung erhält." (It is through relationships, therefore, which derive from the inward essence, that each must make the riches of the others his own. One such character-forming relationship—that is found in the experience of even the crudest nations—is, for example, the relationship between the two sexes. . . . The utility of such relationships for Bildung entirely depends on the extent to which the independence of those in the relationships is maintained at the same time as the intimacy of the relationship.) Wilhelm von Humboldt, *Gesammelte Werke,* vol. 7, ed. Carl Brandes (Berlin: Georg Reimer, 1852), p. 11 (hereafter *Gesammelte Werke*). Humboldt's essay, though written in 1791–1792, was first published in fairly complete form in 1852. See the editor's introduction to Wilhelm von Humboldt, *The Limits of State Action,* ed. J. W. Burrow (Cambridge: Cambridge University Press, 1969), p. vii.

26. "Die wahre Zweck der Menschen, nicht der, welchen die wechselnde Neigung, sondern welchen die ewig unveränderliche Vernunft ihm vorschreibt—ist die höchste und proportionirlichste Bildung seiner Kräfte zu einem Ganzen." (The true end of man, the one prescribed not by changeable inclination but by eternal unalterable reason—is the highest and most harmonious development of his powers to a whole.) Humboldt, *Gesammelte Werke,* p. 10.

27. "Denn der gemeinste Tagelöhner, und der am feinsten Abgebildete muss in seinem Gemüth ursprünglich gleich gestimmt werden, wenn jener nicht unter der Menschenwürde roh, und dieser nicht . . . sentimental, chimärisch, und verschoben werden soll." And a bit later: "Auch Griechisch gelernt zu haben könnte auf diese Weise dem Tischler ebenso wenig unnütz seyn, als Tische zu machen dem Gelehrten." Wilhelm von Humboldt, "Unmaßgebliche Gedanken über den Plan zur Einrichtung des Litthauischen Stadtschulwesens" (Unofficial Reflections on the Plan for the Establishment of the City School System in Lithuania), in Albert Leitzmann, ed., *Wilhelm von Humboldt's Werke*, vol. 13 (Berlin: Behr, 1920), p. 278.

28. "Darin liegt eben der große Fortschritt unserer Zeit, daß sie die Ehre der Arbeit anerkennt, daß sie nicht mehr bloß das Regieren, Malen und Forschen als des anständigen Mannes für würdig erklärt, daß die Handarbeit und Bildung nicht mehr als sich ausschließende Gegensätze kennt." Gustav Schmoller, *Über einige Grundfragen der Sozialpolitik und der Volkswirtschaftslehre*, 2nd ed. (Leipzig: Verlag von Duncker & Humboldt, 1904), pp. 148–149; cited in Philipp Gonon, "George Kerschensteiner and the Plea for Work-Oriented and Vocational Education—Germany's Educational Debates in an Industrial Age," in Mathias Pilz, ed., *The Future of Vocational Education and Training in a Changing World* (Wiesbaden: Springer, 2012), p. 290.

29. Booker T. Washington, *Up from Slavery* (New York: Oxford University Press, 2000; originally published in 1901), p. 71. (I am grateful to an anonymous reviewer for Harvard University Press for drawing this passage to my attention.)

30. Booker T. Washington, "Industrial Education for the Negro," in *The Negro Problem: A Series of Articles by Representative American Negroes of Today* (New York: James Pott & Co., 1903), pp. 20–21.

31. Du Bois, "The Talented Tenth," in Washington et al., *The Negro Problem*, pp. 33–34, 63.

32. "Conservation," p. 44.

33. "Der Einzelne muß sein eigenes Ich vergessen und sich als Glied des Ganzen fühlen; er soll erkennen, wie nichtig sein Leben gegenüber dem Wohl des Ganzen ist." Heinrich von Treitschke, *Politik: Vorlesungen gehalten an der Universität zu Berlin* (Leipzig: Verlag von Hirzel, 1899), p. 74 (hereafter *Politik*).

34. Palmer, *Nature of Goodness*, pp. 172–173. (Chapter VI, where this passage occurs, is entitled "Self-Sacrifice.") The passage first appeared a year earlier in "A Study in Self-Sacrifice," *The Harvard Graduates' Magazine* 11, no. 41 (September 1902): 20. (This was the June 26, 1902, oration to the Phi Beta Kappa chapter at Harvard.) Palmer considers—and rejects—the notion that there is an "identity of interest between society and the individual," that the self-sacrificing individual is "giving up his individuality only through obtaining a larger individuality still" (p. 157). It tells us something about how the Civil War struck this Boston Brahmin that he thought that its loss by his side would have entailed the loss of the country.

35. Josiah Royce, *The Spirit of Modern Philosophy: An Essay in the Form of Lectures* (Boston: Houghton Mifflin, 1892), p. 210.

36. The 1902 lecture was first published in book form in Josiah Royce, *Race Questions, Provincialism, and Other American Problems* (New York: Macmillan, 1908) (hereafter *Provincialism*); the quotes are from pages 61

and 62. Royce was, of course, an attentive reader of Hegel, but other pertinent influences here include Charles Sanders Peirce and his notion of a community of inquirers; see Frances Dickey and M. Jimmie Killingsworth, "Love of Comrades: The Urbanization of Community in Walt Whitman's Poetry and Pragmatist Philosophy," *Walt Whitman Quarterly Review* 21 (Summer 2003): 5. (This essay was kindly drawn to my attention by one of the anonymous reviewers for Harvard University Press.)

37. Josiah Royce, *Philosophy of Loyalty,* ed. John J. McDermott (Nashville: Vanderbilt University Press, 1995), p. 115 (hereafter *Loyalty*).

38. With the critical proviso that "the cause is something which unites many selves in one, and which is therefore in the interest of a community." From Josiah Royce, *The Problem of Christianity* (New York: Macmillan, 1913), p. 68. Reprinted in *Josiah Royce: Selected Writings,* ed. John E. Smith and William Kluback (Mahwah, NJ: Paulist Press, 1988), p. 226.

39. Royce, *Loyalty,* p. 57.

40. *Provincialism,* p. 63. Royce worries, as well, about the "levelling tendency of recent civilization," and how because of the rise of new technologies of communication, along with the consolidation of industries, people tend "to read the same daily news, to share the same general ideas, to submit to the same overmastering social forces, to live in the same external fashions, to discourage individuality, and to approach a dead level of harassed mediocrity." Here we find an almost Millian concern for modern threats to individuality in his work: he worries

about the propensity for assimilation and imitation, along with the rise of a uniform media, because "the result is a tendency to crush the individual." *Provincialism,* pp. 74–75. There was a difference between collective uplift and "the mob spirit."

41. *Dusk of Dawn,* p. 67.

42. "The Souls of White Folk" (1920), in *Writings,* p. 926.

43. See the discussion of Virginia Woolf and Tolstoy in the introduction to my *Cosmopolitanism: Ethics in a World of Strangers* (New York: W. W. Norton, 2005), p. xvi.

44. *Souls,* p. 33; *Dusk of Dawn,* p. 64.

45. "Conservation," pp. 42, 40.

46. *Darkwater,* p. 7. Later, reflecting on how much "what I had called Will and Ability was sheer Luck," he was seized by a great fear: "Was I the masterful captain or the pawn of laughing sprites?" No matter. "I did not hesitate or waver, but just went doggedly to work, and therein lay whatever salvation I have achieved." *Darkwater,* p. 9. He wants to give luck its due, but can't help the nod to will and resolve. And see "Superior Race," p. 60.

47. "Die Natur erklären wir, das Seelenleben verstehen wir." From his 1894 "Ideen über eine beschreibende und zergliedernde Psychologie" (Ideas on a Descriptive and Analytical Psychology), in Wilhelm Dilthey, *Die geistige Welt: Einleitung in die Philosophie des Lebens Gesammelte Schriften* V, ed. G. Misch (Göttingen, Vandenhoeck & Ruprecht, 1990), p. 144; cf. William Dilthey, *Understanding the Human World,* Selected Works, vol. 2, ed. Rudolph A. Makreel and Frithjof Rodi (Princeton: Princeton University Press, 2010), p. 119. See also Michael L. Martin, *Verstehen: The Use of Understanding in Social Science* (New

Brunswick, NJ: Transaction, 2000) (hereafter *Verstehen*), chap. 1 There are obvious affinities with the version of verstehen popularized by Max Weber, but the two conceptions are not identical.

48. Martin, *Verstehen*, p. 10.

49. "Evolving Program," p. 57.

50. *Souls*, pp. 49, 90–91.

51. Kelly Miller, "Radicals and Conservatives," in *Race Adjustment: Essays on the Negro in America*, 2nd ed. (New York: Neale Publishing Co., 1909), pp. 13–29. The quotes are on p. 17.

52. In particular, Dilthey was no subjectivist in the style of the so-called "Lebensphilosophen," of the late nineteen and early twentieth centuries, who took inspiration from Nietzsche and Schopenhauer. In a lecture on "Die Kultur der Gegenwart und die Philosophie" (The Culture of the Present and Philosophy), first given in 1898, he criticized their failure to recognize the fact that they themselves were historical: they did not grasp that "what appears eternal and unconditional from our present perspective is often only the product of a specific culture and epoch." See Frank R. Krummel, *Nietzsche und der deutsche Geist* (Berlin: De Gruyter, 1998), vol. 1, p. 506; and Frederick Beiser, *The German Historicist Tradition* (New York: Oxford University Press, 2011), p. 358.

53. Du Bois, "The Relations of the Negroes to the Whites in the South," *The Annals of the American Academy of Political and Social Sciences* 18 (July 1901): 121–140; reprinted in Dan S. Green and Edwin D. Driver, eds., *W. E. B. Du Bois on Sociology and the Black Community* (Chicago: University of Chicago Press, 1978), p. 266.

CHAPTER THREE: THE CONCEPT OF THE NEGRO

1. "Conservation," p. 39.
2. Ernst Haeckel, "Systematische Übersicht der Zwölf Menschen-Species" (Systematic Overview of the Twelve Human Species), in *Natürliche Schöpfungsgeschichte: Gemeinverständliche wissenschaftliche Vorträge über die Entwicklungslehre im Allgemeinen und diejenige von Darwin, Goethe und Lamarck im Besonderen, über die Anwendung derselben auf den Ursprung des Menschen und andere damit zusammenhängende Grundfragen der Naturwissenschaft* (Natural History of Creation: Popular scientific lectures on the theory of evolution in general and those of Darwin, Goethe and Lamarck in particular, and their application to the origin of humanity and other related fundamental questions of natural science) (Berlin: Georg Reimer 1870; originally published in 1868), p. 626. Haeckel adds to the list in this table—Papuan, Hottentot, Kaffir, Negro, Australian, Malayan, Mongol, Arctic, American, Dravidian, Nubian and Mediterranean (which was his favored way of referring to what others called Caucasians)—a thirteenth item: "Bastarde der Arten," illegitimate offspring of more than one species. Haeckel, being a Darwinian, was a monogenicist in the sense that he thought that all humans had remote common primate ancestors; but he thought the various modern races had evolved separately from earlier nonspeaking primates, which put him on the side of the polygenicists in some debates, since, if humanity was defined by speech, then the various human races had evolved separately. Carl Vogt, *Lectures on Man: His Pace in the Creation, and in the History of the*

Earth, ed. James Hunt, (London: Longman, Green, Longman, and Roberts, 1864), p. 426.

3. "Auf die immer neu entdeckten Rassen unserer Geographen brauchen wir uns hier nicht einzulassen. Dass die Berbern Nordafrikas, die Urbewohner Australiens, die Malaien besondere Rassen bilden, ist sicher; für den Historiker kommen nur die weiße, schwarze, rothe und gelbe Rasse in Betracht." (We need not engage here with the ever newly discovered races of our geographers. That the Berbers of North Africa, the Aboriginals of Australia and the Malays compose specific races, is certain; for the historian only the white, black, red and yellow races come into consideration.) Treitschke, *Politik,* p. 273.

4. Treitschke, *Politik,* p. 276.

5. Treitschke, *Politik,* p. 228.

6. "Conservation," p. 40.

7. "Conservation," p. 41. Notice that I part ways here, at least in emphasis, with the author of "The Uncompleted Argument: Du Bois and the Illusion of Race," *Critical Inquiry* 12 (Autumn 1985). Reprinted in *"Race," Writing and Difference,* ed. Henry Louis Gates Jr. (Chicago: University of Chicago Press, 1986), pp. 21–37.

8. "Conservation," p. 42.

9. Even those who rejected Hegelianism and its Absolute seemed to gravitate toward congruent notions of history and development, as the tongue seeks the missing tooth. Schmoller, as we saw, supposed that an ideal of social justice would progressively be arrived at. For Dilthey, the arrow of history pointed to, well, historicism: *"The historical consciousness of the finitude* of every historical phenomenon and of every human or social state, and of the relativity of every kind of faith, is the final step toward

the liberation of human beings." Wilhelm Dilthey, *Selected Works,* vol. 3: *The Formation of the Historical World in the Human Sciences,* trans. Rudolf A. Makkreel and John Scanlon (Princeton: Princeton University Press, 2002), p. 310.

10. This sort of providential schema was fairly commonplace. The notion that the Negro had a unique gift to give the world can be found in Edward Blyden—see *Christianity, Islam and the Negro Race* (Edinburgh: University of Edinburgh Press, 1967; originally published in 1888)—and, later, in Kelly Miller. See Kelly Miller, "The Artistic Gifts of the Negro," *Voice of the Negro* 3 (April 1906): 252–257 (hereafter "Gifts"), where Miller writes, "The transplanted African made a contribution to the repertoire of song which moistens the eye and melts the heart of the world" ("Gifts," 235). Du Bois was, at times, happy to flirt with the notion of the Negro as spiritually advanced and sensually liberated: "We are the supermen who sit idly by and laugh and look at civilization. We, who frankly want the bodies of our mates and conjure no blush to our bronze cheeks when we own it" ("Superior Race," 599). Shades of Leo Frobenius, the German African explorer, a student of the foundational human geographer Friedrich Ratzel, are evident here. (We will see later that Ratzel influenced Du Bois's thinking about African history.)

11. "A cause is good, not only for me, but for mankind, in so far as it is essentially a *loyalty to loyalty,* that is, an aid and a furtherance of loyalty in my fellows. It is an evil cause in so far as, despite the loyalty that it arouses in me, it is destructive of loyalty in the world of my fellows" Royce, *The Philosophy of Loyalty,* (Nashville: Vanderbilt University Press, 1995; originally published in 1908), p. 56.

12. "Conservation," p. 46. Robert Bernasconi has argued that the talk here of maintaining race identity reflects a preoccupation that came from late nineteenth-century biological speculations about race. In the middle of the century, apologists for Southern slavery like Josiah Nott, had argued that (controversial) census data from the 1840 census showed that African-Americans with European ancestry—Nott, like Du Bois, would have called them mulattos—had higher mortality rates and lower fertility rates than either pure white or pure black people. Nott was rewriting Buffon's idea that species were defined by the absence of fertile offspring, in the face of the evident fact that blacks and whites were, by this criterion, not separate species. Perhaps, Nott thought, if the offspring were merely *less* fertile, that would do. He used this to argue both that there really was a biological reason to avoid race-mixture— miscegenation, as it came to be called—and that there was a biological reality to (because there were these biological effects of) races. So the eventual, if gradual, disappearance of the Negro in a world of racial mixture was a possibility that, in 1897, Du Bois still had to contend with. See Robert L. Bernasconi, "'Our Duty to Conserve': W. E. B. Du Bois's Philosophy of History in Context," *South Atlantic Quarterly* 108 (2009): 519–540, especially pp. 532–533. For a broader discussion of Nott and the related arguments of Frederick L. Hoffman, see George Frederickson, *The Black Image in the White Mind* (Middletown, CT: Wesleyan University Press, 1987), pp. 78–82, 251–253. Recall that in *The Philadelphia Negro*, Du Bois had complained, "In America a census which gives a slight indication of the utter disappearance of

the American Negro from the earth is greeted with ill-concealed delight" (*Philadelphia Negro,* p. 269). Notice that "race identity" here is the identity of the race as a whole, not, like a modern "racial identity," something that individuals have. It is the (whole) race's keeping itself whole that is at issue.

13. "Nationalitäten von so großer Macht und so eigenthümlichen Gepräge, wie die englische, die italienische, sind nicht sowohl Schöpfungen des Landes und der Race, als der großen Abwandlungen der Begebenheiten." Leopold von Ranke, *Weltgeschichte: Ersther Theil. Die älteste historische Völkergruppe und die Griechen* (Leipzig: Duncker und Humboldt, 1881), p. ix. So it is environment not inherited racial character that matters. Ranke's famous claim that the historian should "bloß sagen, wie es eigentlich gewesen" in the preface to his *Geschichte der romanischen und germanischen Völker von 1494 bis 1535* (1824) is discussed in Konrad Regen, "Über Ranke's Diktum von 1824: 'Bloss sagen, wie es eigentlich gewesen,'" *Historisches Jahrbuch* 102 (1982): 439–449. In the late eighteenth century, at the dawn of the modern race concept, Herder spoke dismissively of "so-called races (Rassen)." Michael N. Foster tells us that the term he normally uses for a descent-based group is *Geschlechter,* so *Rassen* is probably an allusion to Kant, who helped inaugurate the discourse with his 1755 essay *Von den Verschiedenen Rassen der Menschen.* (Johann Gottfried Herder, *Philosophical Writings,* ed. Michael N. Foster [Cambridge, MA: Cambridge University Press, 2002], p. 393.)

14. See Zamir, *Dark Voices,* p. 79. Zamir examined Du Bois's economics notebooks in the Du Bois papers at the University of Massachusetts.

15. He conceded that perhaps the "distinction-happy mind of the naturalist" might have been led to do what ordinary people would not. "Gewiß, wenn die Natur nicht den Neger schwarz, den Indianer rot gefärbt hätte, so würde in der ganzen übrigen Organisation diese Stämme zwar vielleicht der sonderungslustige Sinn der Naturforschers, aber nie die Phantasie der Menschen einen Grund gesucht haben, sie als verschiedene Arten zu behandeln und von einem gemeinsamen Ursprünge auszuschließen." (Certainly, if Nature had not colored the Negro black, the Indian red, the imagination of mankind would never have sought in the rest of the organization of these races a reason to treat them as different kinds of men and to deny them common origins, even if perhaps that would have been the inclination of the distinction-happy mind of the naturalist.) Hermann Lotze, *Microkosmos: Ideen zur Naturgeschichte und Geschichte der Menschheit* (Microcosmus: Ideas Concerning Man the Natural History and the History of Humanity,* vol. 2 (Leipzig: Felix Meiner, 1923), p. 117 (hereafter *Microcosmus*).

16. "Gesetzt, es wäre dokumentarisch nachweisbar, daß die Ureltern der Neger wirklich wahre unzweifelhafte Affen gewesen, aber es bliebe auch gleichzeitig bei der Tatsache, daß diese jetzigen Neger aufrechtgehen, sprechen, denken und überhaupt die Intelligenz, sei sie groß oder klein, besitzen, welche ihnen erfahrungsmäßig zukommt: welche sittliche Entschuldigung gäbe es dann für die Grausamkeit, ihre Behandlung nicht nach dem einzurichten, was sie sind, sondern nach dem, was ihre Ureltern waren, oder Logisch ausgedruckt, nach der Art oder Spezies, zu welcher sie ihrer Herkunft nach gehören? Oder wenn es nun umgekehrt feststände, daß die

Affen verkümmerte Menschen seien, deren Voreltern wir vielleicht noch in der Geschichte vergangener Zeiten in menschlicher Gestalt antreffen, es bliebe aber gleichzeitig dabei, daß sie jetzt eben durchaus nur wirkliche Affen sind?" (Suppose it were verifiable through documents, that the ancestors of the Negro really were true indubitable apes, but the fact also remained at the same time, that these present-day Negroes were possessed of intelligence, be it great or small, and of the capacity to walk upright, to speak and to think (which we know from experience they are): what moral excuse would there be for the cruelty of not treating them according to what they are, but according to what their ancestors were—or, to put the matter logically, according to the kind or species to which they belong by their ancestry? Or, if it now were certain, conversely, that the apes were stunted human beings, whose ancestors we perhaps meet in human form in the history of past times, would it not still remain the case, that they now are nevertheless only really apes?) *Microcosmus*, p. 135.

17. "Denn ganz gewöhnlich beginnt man diese Überlegungen mit der Behauptung, es sei vor allem nötig, den Begriff einer natürlichen Art oder Spezies und den einer Spielart oder Varietät so genau als möglich festzustellen. Man sucht den Satz zu begründen, dass die Menschenrassen nur Spielarten einer Art nicht verschiedene Arten einer Gattung sind." (For it is quite normal to begin these considerations with the assertion that is it necessary above all to establish as precisely as possible the concept of a natural kind [Art] or species and a variant [Spielart] or variety. One then seeks to establish the proposition that human races are only variants [Spielarten] of one

species [Art] not different species [Arten] of one genus.) *Microcosmus*, p. 132. While *Art* and *Gattung* are used in biological contexts to mean *species* and *genus*, the word *Art* can still just mean *sort* or *kind*, and *Gattung* can mean just *class* or *category*. So in Lotze's German the thought that there is a fair amount of loose talk here is even more plausible. "unter einem logischen Formelspiel verschwinden zu lassen." (allow it to turn into a logical game of formulas.) *Microcosmus*, p. 132. "Varietät ist . . . ein Titel ohne Einkünfte." (Variety is . . . a title without emoluments.) *Microcosmus*, p. 133. The image here, presumably, is one of being ennobled without an estate! "Diese Begriffe und alle Versuche zu ihrer genauen Definition entscheiden daher nichts; das einzige reelle Objekt der Untersuchung, auf welches man diese logische Weitläufigkeiten hartnäckig immer wieder zurückfuhren muß, besteht nur in der einen Aufgabe, äußere Bedingungen nicht bloß im Unbestimmten ahnen zu lassen, sondern namhaft zu machen, aus denen historisch und wo möglich experimentell die Umwandlung einer Rassenform in eine andere beweisbar wird." (These concepts and all attempts at a precise definition of them therefore settle nothing; the only real object of investigation, to which these logical prolixities must persistently be brought back again and again, consists in the task not just of vaguely conjecturing about, but of making it possible to name external conditions out of which the transformation of one race form into another is historically and—where possible— experimentally provable.) *Microcosmus*, p. 134.

18. *Dusk of Dawn*, p. 26.

19. "Wenn die Natur Grenzen zwischen den einzelnen Gattungen ihrer Geschöpfe innehalten will, muß es irgendwo

eine Verschiedenheit der Gestaltungstriebe geben, welche die Erzeugungen von Mittelformen ausschließt." *Microcosmus*, p. 133.

20. "Die Kreuzung von Weißen und Negern in den Mulatten, die von Weißen und Indianern in den Mestizen bringt häufig, namentlich aber durch später wiederholte Verbindung dieser Mischlinge mit dem weißen Stamme, sehr schöne, auch geistig wohlbegabte Bildungen hervor." (The crossing of whites and blacks in mulattoes, [or] of whites with Indians in mestizos, often produces—especially after later repeated combination of these half-breeds with the white strain—a very attractive, and intellectually (geistig) talented constitution.) *Microcosmus* pp. 131–132.

21. "Fast überall sehen wir die Neigung, die neue syntaktische Würde der Worte in eine neue metaphysische Würde ihres Inhaltes umzudeuten." (Almost everywhere we see the inclination to find a novel interpretation of the new syntactic dignity of words in a new metaphysical dignity for their contents.) *Microcosmus*, p. 250; "In allen diesen Fällen schafft uns die Sprache eine Mythologie . . ." *Microcosmus*, p. 630.

22. Hermann Lotze, *System of Philosophy Part I: Logic in Three Books, Of Thought, Of Investigation and of Knowledge,* ed. Bernard Bosanquet, trans. R. L. Nettleship (Oxford: Clarendon Press, 1884), pp. 486–487.

23. Compare John Dupré's "promiscuous realism" in *The Disorder of Things* (Cambridge, MA: Harvard University Press, 1993); and Philip Kitcher's suggestion that "really promiscuous realism drops the realism and becomes pragmatism" in his "Does 'Race' Have a Future?," in *Preludes to Pragmatism: Toward a Reconstruction of Philosophy* (New York: Oxford University Press, 2012), p. 151.

24. Wilhelm Dilthey, *Selected Works*, vol. 1: *Introduction to the Human Sciences*, ed. Rudolf A. Makkreel and Frithjof Rodi (Princeton: Princeton University Press, 1991), p. 92 (hereafter *Selected Works*). As the editors remark, Dilthey uses the word *Nation* here "pejoratively as a term with a mystical meaning." His own preference is for the word *Volk*.

25. "Conservation," p. 40.

26. Dilthey, *Selected Works*, p. 91. For a valuable discussion of Dilthey and Herder, see Frederick C. Beiser, *The German Historicist Tradition* (New York: Oxford University Press, 2012), pp. 99 et seq.

27. Axel Schäfer suggests that Schmoller, by emphasizing the transformative effects of social and economic arrangements, led Du Bois toward a more "dynamic conception of race." Schäfer, "German Social Thought," p. 935. "Du Bois's abandonment of the belief in fixed racial attributes and his embrace of the notion that the true meaning of black culture would reveal itself only in the process of social interaction and participation were not the result of his disillusionment with German thought, but an integral part of the social ideas gleaned from his mentor Gustav Schmoller." Schäfer, "German Social Thought," p. 939.

28. *Select Discussion of Race Problems: A Collection of Papers of Especial Use in Study of Negro American Problems; with the Proceedings of the Twentieth Annual Conference for Study of Negro Problems, held at Atlanta University, May 24, 1915*, ed. J. A. Bigham, Atlanta University Publications, no. 20 (Atlanta: Atlanta University Press, 1916). Boas's Commencement Address is excerpted as "Old African Civilizations," pp. 83–85.

29. Du Bois's "Races of Men" is reproduced in *Select Discussion of Race Problems*, pp. 17–24, from the 1906 proceed-

ings of the Atlanta Conference (hereafter "Races of Men"). This quote is from p. 23.

30. "Races of Men," pp. 20–21.

31. For a lucid discussion of these issues see Luigi Luca Cavalli-Sforza, Paolo Menozzi, and Alberto Piazza, *The History and Geography of Human Genes* (Princeton: Princeton University Press, 1996).

32. "Races of Men," p. 13. This claim was prompted by *Papers in Inter-Racial Problems Communicated to the First Universal Races Congress Held at the University of London,* July 26–29, 1911, ed. G. Spiller (London: P. S. King & Son; Boston, World's Peace Foundation, 1911).

33. Charles Darwin, *The Descent of Man and Selection in Relation to Sex,* vol. 1 (New York: Appleton and Co, 1871), p. 217.

34. He went on, in language with a Marxian hue, "There are great groups,—now with common history, now with common interests, now with common ancestry; more and more common experience and present interest drive back the common blood and the world today consists, not of races, but of the imperial commercial group of master capitalists, international and predominantly white; the national middle classes of the several nations, white, yellow, and brown, with strong blood bonds, common languages, and common history; the international laboring class of all colors; the backward, oppressed groups of nature-folk, predominantly yellow, brown, and black." *Darkwater,* pp. 47–48.

35. *Dusk of Dawn,* p. 137.

36. *Dusk of Dawn,* pp. 137–138.

37. Du Bois, "The Dilemma of the Negro," *American Mercury* (October 1924): 181.

38. *Darkwater,* p. 11.

39. Jean-Paul Sartre, *Anti-Semite and Jew,* trans. George Joseph Becker (New York: Schocken, 1948), p. 143; Du Bois quote from Beck, "Study Abroad Student"; Frantz Fanon, *Black Skin, White Mask,* trans. Richard Philcox (New York: Grove, 2008; first published in France in 1952), p. 93.

40. *Darkwater,* p. 100.

41. *Darkwater,* p. 99.

CHAPTER FOUR: THE MYSTIC SPELL

1. Countee Cullen, "Heritage," in *The New Negro,* ed. Alain Locke (New York: Touchstone, 1997), p. 250.

2. W. E. B. Du Bois, *John Brown* (New York: Oxford University Press, 2007; originally published in 1909), p. 1.

3. G. W. F. Hegel, *The Philosophy of History,* trans. J. Sibree (New York: The Colonial Press, 1999), p. 99 (hereafter *Philosophy of History*).

4. Hegel, *Philosophy of History.*

5. W. E. B. Du Bois, *Black Folk, Then and Now* (New York, Oxford University Press, 2007; originally published in 1939), p. xxxi (hereafter *Black Folk*).

6. *Black Folk,* p. xxxi.

7. Such attitudes persisted into the 1960s; see Kwame Anthony Appiah, "Africa: The Hidden History," *The New York Review of Books* 45, no. 20 (December 17, 1998): 64–72.

8. W. E. B. Du Bois, *The Negro Church: Report of a Social Study Made under the Direction of Atlanta University; together with the Proceedings of the Eighth Conference for the Study of the Negro Problems, held at Atlanta University, May 26, 1903,* ed. W. E. Burghardt Du Bois (Atlanta: The Atlanta University Press, 1903), http://docsouth.unc.edu/church/negro church/dubois.html, accessed July 10, 2013.

9. W. E. B. Du Bois, *The World and Africa & Color and De-mocracy* (New York: Oxford University Press, 2007; origi-nally published in 1947 and in 1945, respectively), p. 50 (hereafter *The World and Africa*). For a fine (and gener-ous) survey of Du Bois's African history by a distin-guished modern African historian, see Robin Law, "Du Bois as a Pioneer of African History: A Reassessment of The Negro (1915)," in Mary Keller and Chester J. Fon-tenot Jr., eds., *Re-cognizing W. E. B. Du Bois in the Twenty-First Century* (Macon, GA: Mercer University Press, 2007), pp. 14–33.

10. *The Negro,* (1915), p. 4.

11. *The Negro* (1915), p. 6.

12. *The Negro* (1915), p. 7.

13. *The Negro* (1915). Herder, in his *Outlines of a Philosophy of the History of Man,* reports a similar theory. He notes that the only part of the Negro that's black is "the retic-ular membrane beneath the cuticle, which is common to all, and even in us, at least in, some parts, and under certain circumstances, is more or less coloured. Camper has demonstrated this; and according to him we all have the capacity of becoming negroes" (pp. 266–267). This identification of Africa with racial mixture pre-supposes, at least in principle, some pure races to be mixing; and Du Bois never seems to have grasped that the biology he was learning meant that there were no pure biological races, precisely because of the constant flow of genes across the boundaries of geographical populations.

14. *The Negro* (1915), p. 25.

15. *The Negro* (1915), p. 9.

16. *The Negro* (1915).

17. Herodotus's account has since been subjected to skeptical scrutiny. Alan B. Lloyd, "Necho and the Red Sea: Some Considerations," *Journal of Egyptian Archaeology* 63, (1977): 142–155.

18. *The Negro* (1915), p. 21.

19. *Black Folk*, p. 10.

20. David E. Bloom and Jeffrey D. Sachs, "Geography, Demography and Economic Growth in Africa" (Cambridge, MA: Harvard Institute for International Development, October 1998), http://www.cid.harvard.edu/archive/malaria/docs/brookafr.pdf, accessed July 10, 2013.

21. *Black Folk*, p. 273.

22. *Black Folk*.

23. *The World and Africa*, p. 27.

24. *The World and Africa*, p. 164.

25. This observation is usually attributed to the Augustan historian of the Roman republic, Dionysius of Halicarnassus—after Herodotus, the most famous historian to have been born in that Ionian city. But the *Ars Rhetorica* from which it comes is now attributed to someone else.

26. "Frobenius is not popular among conventional historians or anthropologists," Du Bois wrote, "but he was a great man and a great thinker. He looked upon Africa with unprejudiced eyes and has been more valuable for the interpretation of the Negro than any other man I know." *The World and Africa*, x–xi.

27. *Autobiography*, p. 102.

28. It's a dream that persisted. In "My Negro Problem—and Ours," published in the last year of Du Bois's life, Norman Podhoretz writes, "I think I know why the Jews once wished to survive (though I am less certain as to

why we still do): they not only believed that God had given them no choice, but they were tied to a memory of past glory and a dream of imminent redemption. What does the American Negro have that might correspond to this? His past is a stigma, his color is a stigma, and his vision of the future is the hope of erasing the stigma by making color irrelevant, by making it disappear as a fact of consciousness. I share this hope, but I cannot see how it will ever be realized unless color does in fact disappear: and that means not integration, it means assimilation, it means—let the brutal word come out— miscegenation . . . the wholesale merging of the two races." *Commentary* (February 1963): 101.

29. *Dusk of Dawn,* pp. 65–66. I don't want to reduce Du Bois's scholarly engagement with Africa, let alone his Pan-African activism, to a mode of self-exploration: he was a committed foe of colonialism and imperialism. He plausibly took his books about Africa to be part of a project of uplift. But Africa was not the solution to his perplexities of "race identity." And its cultures, he supposed toward the end of his life, were as much a burden as a gift: "Great Goethe sang, 'Entbehren sollst du, sollst entbehren'—'Thou shalt forego, shalt do without.' If Africa unites it will be because each part, each nation, each tribe gives up a part of its heritage for the good of the whole. That is what union means; that is what Pan-Africa means. . . . Your local tribal, much-loved languages must yield to the few world tongues which serve the largest numbers of people and promote understanding and world literature." Africa's political weakness had allowed it to be harrowed by white industrial capitalism, the aging Du Bois believed. What the continent needed,

he felt, was a strong dose of modernity and efficiency. (A sentiment shared by Richard Wright in his *Black Power: A Record of Reactions in a Land of Pathos* [New York: Harper and Brothers, 1954]; see my "A Long Way From Home: Richard Wright in the Gold Coast," in *Richard Wright*, ed. Harold Bloom [New York: Chelsea House, Modern Critical Views, 1987], pp. 173–190.) Critics on the left have, in their readings of Du Bois, been especially disappointed in this development. Adolph Reed Jr. refers to "the flippancy with which Du Bois dispatched intra-African particularity" as evidence of "the centrality of the universalist and homogenizing assumptions of social engineering in his thinking." *W. E. B. Du Bois and American Political Thought: Fabianism and the Color Line* (New York: Oxford University Press, 1997), p. 81. And see Kenneth Mostern's lively discussion in his *Autobiography and Black Identity Politics* (Cambridge: Cambridge University Press, 1999), pp. 68–76, which focuses on Du Bois's putative defections from, and discomfort with, his blackness.

CHAPTER FIVE: THE ONE AND THE MANY

1. "Evolving Program," p. 58. He had struck similar chords earlier. Writing in "Sociology Hesitant" (1905 ms.; first published in *boundary 2* 27, no. 3 [2000]: 37–44) Du Bois affirms the anti-positivist, neo-Kantian creed. Real sociologists "have refused to cloud their reason with metaphysical entities undiscovered and undiscoverable, and they have also refused to neglect the greatest possible field of scientific investigation because they are unable to find laws similar to the law of gravitation. They have

assumed a world of physical law peopled by beings capable in some degree of actions inexplicable and uncalculable according to these laws. And their object has been to determine as far as possible the limits of the Uncalculable—to measure, if you will, the Kantian Absolute and Undetermined Ego." "Evolving Program," p. 42.

2. *Dusk of Dawn*, pp. 86–87.

3. The aim, in surveying those "uncharted lands," was to advance to an outlook that is "rational and consistent with the best interests of the whole world of men." *Dusk of Dawn*, pp. 86–87. Some scholars seem to think that Du Bois had to choose between James and Royce—that his soul had to belong either to the idealist or to the pragmatist camp. James did look askance at Royce's version of the Absolute, which he took to be inconsistent with true freedom; and Royce chastised the "relativity of truth" he thought James courted. There is that "Battle of the Absolute." But Royce's argument for the Absolute Knower was exactly the fact that any of our statements might be in error; and James's individualism was more social than it sometimes appears. Their pairing has as many complementary aspects as contradictory ones.

4. Josiah Royce, *The Problem of Christianity,* vol. 2 (New York: Macmillan, 1913), pp. 50, 51.

5. As W. B. Gallie wrote in introducing the term, essentially contestable terms are those whose "proper use inevitably involves endless disputes about their proper use on the part of users." W. B. Gallie, "Essentially Contested Concepts," *Proceedings of the Aristotelian Society* 56 (1956): 169.

6. See Quentin Skinner, "The Idea of a Cultural Lexicon," *Essays in Criticism* 29, no. 3 (1979): 205–224; and "Meaning

and Understanding in the History of Ideas," *History and Theory* 8, no. 1 (1969): 3–53. The expression "race identity" in the late nineteenth century refers primarily to the identity of a race—to what makes the group what it is—not to the racial component of an individual self, a member of the race; as in: "At the close of the rebellion it was expected that the negro race would gradually disperse throughout the United States, and lose its race identity and distinct habitat." Charles Shearer Keyser, *Minden Armais, the Man of the New Race* (Philadelphia: American Printing House, 1890), p. 93. In this usage it's possible to talk about the race identity of an individual, but only to raise the question of what race a person belongs to, not to refer to some racial characteristics he or she has; as here, when Anna Julia Cooper discusses Martin Delany in 1892: "The late Martin R. Delany, who was an unadulterated black man, used to say when the honors of state fell upon him, that when he entered the council of kings the black race entered with him; meaning, I suppose, that there was no discounting his race identity and attributing his achievements to some admixture of Saxon blood." Anna Julia Cooper, *A Voice from the South* (New York: Oxford University Press, 1988; originally published in 1892), p. 30.

7. William James, *The Principles of Psychology* (New York: Henry Holt, 1890), p. 294 (hereafter *Psychology*). James Campbell links James's "social selves" analysis to Du Bois's double-consciousness; see James Campbell, "Du Bois and James," *Transactions of the Charles S. Peirce Society* 28, no. 3 (Summer 1992): 573–574.

8. James, *Psychology*, p. 295.

9. James wrote, "The ideal social self which I thus seek in appealing to their decision may be very remote: it may

be represented as barely possible. I may not hope for its realization during my lifetime; I may even expect the future generations, which would approve me if they knew me, to know nothing about me when I am dead and gone. Yet still the emotion that beckons me on is indubitably the pursuit of an ideal social self, of a self that is at least *worthy* of approving recognition by the highest *possible* judging companion, if such companion there be. . . . All progress in the social Self is the substitution of higher tribunals for lower; this ideal tribunal is the highest; and most men, either continually or occasionally, carry a reference to it in their breast. The humblest outcast on this earth can feel himself to be real and valid by means of this higher recognition." James, *Psychology,* pp. 315–316.

10. Mead published little during his life; his best known work, *Mind, Self, and Society,* was assembled from student notes from a course he taught on social psychology, 1927–1930 (*Mind, Self, and Society: From the Standpoint of a Social Behaviorist,* ed. Charles W. Morris [Chicago: University of Chicago Press, 1967] [hereafter *Mind, Self, and Society*]). Another volume, *The Individual and the Social Self,* edited by David L. Miller (Chicago: University of Chicago Press, 1982), is taken, in part, from student notes from a course dating to 1912. Many of his arguments evolved over the years in courses he had taught at Chicago since the mid-1890s, but dating the evolution of his thought can be tricky.

11. Mead, *Mind, Self, and Society,* pp. 158, 154, 133, 262.

12. Mead, *Mind, Self, and Society,* section 18, "The Self and the Organism," pp. 135–143.

13. Mead, *Mind, Self, and Society,* p. 175.

14. He went on, "We are realizing ourselves as members of a larger community. The vivid nationalism of the present period should, in the end, call out an international attitude of the larger community." Mead, *Mind, Self, and Society,* p. 265. Note that an early version of his "I"/ "me" distinction is rehearsed in Mead, "The Definition of the Psychical," in *The Decennial Publications of the University of Chicago* (Chicago: University of Chicago Press, 1903), p. 104.

15. *The Philosophy of Loyalty,* p. 107.

16. "The Name 'Negro,'" *The Crisis* (March 1928): 96–97. This is a reply to a letter from Roland A. Barton, a high school sophomore in South Bend, Indiana. Du Bois concludes, mischievously, that "a Negro by any other name would be just as black and just as white." Du Bois may or may not have been making a point when he misspelled Roland Barton's name in his reply. Reprinted in Julius Lester, ed., *The Seventh Son: The Thought and Writings of W. E. B. Du Bois,* vol. 2 (New York: Vintage, 1971), pp. 55.

17. *Souls,* p. 52.

18. *Dusk of Dawn,* p. 86.

19. Ernest Renan, *Qu'est-ce qu'une nation?,* 2nd ed. (Paris: Calmann-Lévy, 1882).

20. *Dusk of Dawn,* pp. 70, 71, 67.

21. Du Bois, "Immortality," in Sydney Strong, ed., *We Believe in Immortality: Affirmations by One Hundred Men and Women* (New York: Coward-McCann, 1929), p. 18; reprinted in David Levering Lewis, ed., *W. E. B. Du Bois: A Reader* (New York: Henry Holt and Co., 1995), p. 134.

22. "The Last Message of Dr. W. E. B. Du Bois to the World," *The Journal of Negro History* 49, no. 2 (April 1964): 145.

23. Josiah Royce, *The Basic Writings of Josiah Royce,* ed. John J. McDermot (New York: Fordham University Press, 2005), pp. 965–967.

ACKNOWLEDGMENTS

When the Department of African-American and African Studies at Harvard invited me to give the Du Bois Lectures, I was greatly honored. These lectures, though named for Dr. W. E. B. Du Bois, are supposed to address some topic in the vast range of topics that interested him. There is no obligation to address the man himself. But this was, I found, exactly what I most wanted to do. I was pleased to have the opportunity to think, once more, about the life and work of this preeminent American intellectual. My first work in the field of African-American Studies was about Du Bois, and the way he struggled to think about race over the first half of the twentieth century—and everything I have done in the field has been inspired by his extraordinary example.

I was delighted, too, to be returning not only to a department that had been, for more than a decade, a most hospitable home for me, but also to one of his almae matres. And a pleasure it indeed was, over three days in November 2010, to explore some of the themes in the work of this most fascinating and accomplished of scholars with so many people who share an engagement with his work. So I must begin by thanking the department for this honor and this opportunity. I am grateful, too, to all those with whom I have discussed Du Bois over these many years, in conversations too numerous to count and too extensive to recall. Among my interlocutors during these years, though, I should like to thank by name Henry Louis Gates Jr., Robert Gooding-Williams, Jorge Gracia, Evelyn Brooks Higginbotham, Lucius Outlaw, and Tommie Shelby; and I must also thank the many students in courses where I have discussed Du Bois's work, at Yale, Cornell, Duke, Harvard, and Princeton. As usual, I offer my thanks to those who may recognize thoughts they shared with me over the years, even if my memory has not recovered them. I am conscious that I, too, live in a rich matrix of ideas.

I began to think about the topic of this book when I was asked to give a Du Bois lecture at the Humboldt University in May 2005, in the Senate Hall where Du Bois had been honored half a century earlier. I tried out a version a month earlier in a talk to the students of the Columbia University Core Program in the Humanities, and a year later as the first

James Baldwin lecture at Princeton and at a conference at the University of Virginia. Since then, audiences at Grinnell College and the University of Chicago have heard developing versions of my thoughts. After the Du Bois Lectures at Harvard, I tried out a close-to-final version of one part of the argument as the first Henry Louis Gates Jr. lecture at Yale. I am grateful to those who made suggestions at all these great colleges and universities as my understanding morphed and mutated; and also to two anonymous readers for Harvard University Press, whose suggestions were most useful. I'm especially grateful, as always, to Henry Finder, my spouse, for his probing interrogations.

I have recorded the written sources I have relied on most in the notes, but a bibliography of everything I have read about Du Bois would be too vast an appendage to this essay. One work, however, deserves mentioning above all, because all of us who think about Du Bois owe its author a great debt. It is David Levering Lewis's magisterial two-volume biography: *W. E. B. Du Bois, 1868–1919: Biography of a Race* (New York: Henry Holt, 1994) and *W. E. B. Du Bois, 1919–1963: The Fight for Equality and the American Century* (New York: Henry Holt, 2000).

I am very conscious that my own engagement with these issues follows in Du Bois's footsteps. Questions about cosmopolitanism, the Negro, and Africa are central to my own identity. And although I made my journey in the opposite direction, beginning in Ghana and ending here in the United States as an American, I have lived my life in much the same geography—both physical and intellectual—that shaped this great Ghanaian-American. My family—spread as it is over the three continents that formed Du Bois—is itself (among many other things, no doubt) a small sampling of the African Diaspora. Each of them will recognize here and there a thought that belongs to the history we share. This book is for them all.

INDEX